TECTONIC ART
Ancient Trade Guilds and Companies
Free Masons' Guilds

Clement E. Stretton

With foreword by Paul Mycock
1st Grand Master Mason of the Worshipful Society of Free Masons, Rough Masons, Wallers, Slaters, Paviors, Plaisterers and Bricklayers (The Operatives)

First published 2023

ISBN 978 0 85318 644 1

All rights reserved. No part of this book may be reproduced or transmitted in any form or by any means, electronic or mechanical, including photocopying, recording, scanning or by any information storage and retrieval system, on the internet or elsewhere, without permission from the Publisher in writing.

© Lewis Masonic 2023

Design, layout and typesetting by Jason Mayfield-Lewis

Published by Lewis Masonic
166 Great North Road, Eaton Socon, St Neots, Cambridgeshire PE19 8EH

Printed in England.

Visit the Lewis Masonic website at www.lewismasonic.co.uk

Copyright
Illegal copying and selling of publications deprives authors, publishers and booksellers of income, without which there would be no investment in new publications. Unauthorised versions of publications are also likely to be inferior in quality and contain incorrect information. You can help by reporting copyright infringements and acts of piracy to the Publisher or the UK Copyright Service.

Images
Scans of the original source material provided by The Museum of Freemasonry, London and Hallamshire College Book Collection.

Publisher's Note

When reproducing a historical work there are always questions concerning how close to the original source the designer should remain. Having already decided to include the scans of the primary material for those readers interested in being able to see how it was originally produced, the designer and myself concluded that the priority for the transcription should be readability. Therefore, we departed from the narrow columns used in the original format which allowed us to use a larger font. However, we chose to remain faithful to the original in terms of the text itself as we felt that some of the idiosyncrasies found throughout gave the text its character and were in some ways the voice of Clement Stretton himself.

It seems to be a rule that when reproducing a historical work there must be an unforeseen hurdle to overcome. For this project it was after the designer had carefully edited and laid out the work that we realised several pages were missing. Assuming this to be an error during the scanning process, we contacted The Museum of Freemasonry in London only to find they were missing from the original too! Having already put so much work in, we were reluctant to let the project fall by the wayside and a great search for another copy began. We are thankful to Dr John Wade and Calum Heaton of The Hallamshire College Book Collection who kindly assisted in finding and sending us photographs of the missing pages.

Kindra Faulks

Lewis Masonic

Back by popular demand!

The decision to publish Tectonic Art came about after several requests for the text to be made available. Originally the text was a transcript of a talk that Clement Stretton, the Founder of the Worshipful Society of Operative Masons, gave for the Leicester Association of Engineers in 1909. The talk was so popular and so many people were asking for copies of what was said that the Melton Mowbray Times decided it would be worthwhile printing it as a booklet, which was sold for a shilling. Now after all this time once again demand has caused Lewis Masonic to produce a new edition of the book, and once you start to read it I am sure you will understand why.

This book is a fantastic introduction for those with an interest in Operative Freemasonry giving a fascinating history of the guilds, the roles of Square and Arch Masons and an overview of the system we preserve in our order. It also provides a great deal of context to the ritual both in the Constitution Ceremony and in the Lecture of the VI Degree.

Readers who are members of The Worshipful Society of Free Masons, Rough Masons, Wallers, Slaters, Paviors, Plaisterers and Bricklayers will notice some subtle (and not so subtle!) differences in the terminology used in this text, it having been written when the society was still taking form.

This book has been out of print since its publication and although the text has appeared in some academic journals this is the first time it has been available to purchase. It is hoped that this and other texts from those who founded the order and helped preserve the ancient traditions of Operative Masonry will lead to more research into our past and awareness of the valuable teachings of our tradition.

Paul Mycock

1st Grand Master Mason of the Worshipful Society of Free Masons, Rough Masons, Wallers, Slaters, Paviors, Plaisterers and Bricklayers (The Operatives)

Author's Note.

For thousands of years Guilds in general and the Free Masons' Guild in particular, carried out the most strict letter of the law, not to allow outsiders to obtain the very "least trace" of the Ancient system of working, but a few years ago at a meeting held at York it was decided that it was perfectly lawful to give certain "bare facts" on condition that the proposed article or communication be first sent to the proper Officer for his "mark of approval."

During the past few years a number of interesting visits, have been paid to quarries, Iron works, Coal mines and Engineering works in or near Leicestershire, and at several of the quarries much interest was taken in the fact that although the work was not being carried out under the Guild system, many of the workmen "proved themselves by proper signs" to be members of the Ancient Operative Masons' Guild, which system has come down to us from Babylon.

When the writer was first asked to draw up a paper on Operative Masonry he feared that it would be impossible to write anything of interest without running the risk of saying too much. However, after consultation with a Grand Master Mason the work was undertaken.

When the M.S. was completed it was duly forwarded to the proper Officer, and came back with the necessary "mark of approval" and very highly commended, as "the best thing that had been written upon this subject."

On the 20th, February last the paper was read before the Leicester Association of Engineers, at their meeting held at the Technical School, Leicester, and the reports of the same have appeared in the "Melton Mowbray Times" for March 12th and 26th April 2nd, 9th and 16th.

Naturally it is pleasing to the writer to find that the articles have proved of so much public interest that they are to be reproduced in the present pamphlet form.

Saxe Coburg House,
    Leicester, April 19th, 1909.

CLEMENT E. STRETTON,
    (Masons' Guild, 7th degree).

TECTONIC ART.

Ancient Trade Guilds and Companies.
Free Masons' Guilds.
By CLEMENT E. STRETTON.

TRADE Guilds, Castes, Societies, Companies and similar institutions have existed from a very remote but unknown period in the world's history, and a reference to Whitaker's Almanack will show that in London alone there are fully eighty of these ancient trade companies still in existence at the present day.

The Lord Mayor of London is always selected from the members of one or other of these City Livery Companies, and it is a well-known fact that a copy of every book printed in this country, for sale, has by law to be forwarded to the Stationers' Company at their Stationers' Hall, London.

The origin of all the trade guilds, many thousands of years ago, was the desire of each trade to keep its particular art, science, knowledge, method, system or craft in its own hands, in other words to strictly preserve the respective "trade secrets."

Experts who have made investigations amongst the ruins of Babylon have been able to obtain proof from the ancient inscriptions and marks, that the Guild system for all trades was in use at the time when that city was built, also that the King of Babylon, Nimrod, was either a Grand Master or a Protector of every trade guild.

All the guilds which work in metal, in all parts of the world, in their "Traditional History" state that

> "Tubal-Cain founded the smith-craft of gold, silver, iron, copper, bronze, steel, and other metals."

The Building Guilds have records that

> "Jabal founded the craft of geometry and first wrought houses of stone."

The Weavers' Guilds claim that

> "Naamah founded the craft of weaving."

The Musicians' Guild states that

> "Jubal was the father of all such as handle the harp and the organ, and the craft of music and song of mouth."

To carry out its system each trade guild divided its methods and also its members into grades or degrees, and the officers and workmen were instructed in that particular portion of the art or craft which belonged to the respective degree of which they were members, consequently it will be evident that to obtain the full knowledge of any trade a person must begin as an apprentice in the lowest grade and by skill and attention to duty, gradually "work up" to be a Master or chief ruler of his Guild.

The number of grades or degrees varied according to the practical requirements of the trade, but in each instance it follows that if a young man desired to work in any of the trades he must belong to the Trade Guild, as the members would neither teach nor work with any "outsider."

The young man must seek and find the respective Trades Hall and make formal application to be made an apprentice to the trade, and bring at least seven persons who must satisfy a master or other officials as to his good character; also that he has not previously been an apprentice to any other guild, and that he has never been discharged or expelled or left the work without authority. His application having in due time been received and accepted he attended at the proper time to go through the formal ceremony of being "apprenticed."

The "proper time" in every case was twelve o'clock at noon on the last day of the week, that being the only time when "apprentices" were "made." Every guild required the candidate to "Fear God, honour the King, obey the ancient charges, and strictly preserve the secrets of the trade."

Having been sworn, and "charged," his name was entered upon the roll of apprentices. He was then provided with the proper working tools used in the trade, being carefully taught and instructed how to use them. He was always addressed as Brother, and officially described as "an entered apprentice to the craft of—" (in accordance with the name of the trade).

After the "Day of Rest" the apprentice commenced regular work, being placed with the other new hands in the lowest room, yard, or degree, where they were all under the special control of expert members of the craft or calling.

Gradually the young apprentice progressed, and was promoted to higher work and rank in exact accordance with his skill, knowledge and ability, and in time it was open to him to attain to the highest office in his guild.

"Efficiency"—the power, skill, knowledge and will to perform the allotted task, whatever it might be, in a proper workmanlike manner, was the object and desire of every guild member; therefore, to say that a person was a master of his craft was an honour to him.

The particulars above given show the general outline which applied, and still applies, to all the ancient guilds in all parts of the world, and attention must now be directed to

THE GUILD SYSTEM OF WORKING.

In the construction of any building of importance it follows that the members of many guilds must be employed, and consequently it is of very great importance that the chief officers of each guild should be perfectly well acquainted with the particular portion of the work which each has to perform and carry out.

As an instance, let it be assumed that a very important building be required, such as a temple at Jerusalem.

The first step towards the erection of such an edifice was to decide upon the "unit of measure" to be adopted, and, secondly, to have a complete model constructed to scale, showing every part of the building and its fittings made in the proper material. In ancient times each nation had two standard units of measure. The one was the unit for ordinary use and for civil purposes, the other was the Royal measure, used for ecclesiastical buildings, temples, kings' palaces, and the most important structures.

For instance the Hebrews at Jerusalem had a short cubit for general use based upon the length of a man's arm from the elbow to the tip of the middle finger, or very nearly equal to our modern 18 inches. They also had a Royal cubit which is clearly explained by *Ezekiel xl. 5*, who shows that the Royal or long cubit was a short "cubit and an hand breadth," therefore it follows that the Royal cubit was equal to our 1.824 English foot, or very similar to the present 21 7-8th inches.

This long cubit was divided into 60 minutes in length, each being very similar to our 3-8ths of an inch, each minute being again divided into 60 parts known as seconds.

If we refer to the volume of the S.L. *II. Chronicles iii. 3*, it will be found that King David instructed Solomon when building the temple to adopt "The length by cubits after the first measure." The word here translated in the English Bible as "first" should read "first importance" or the Royal measure.

In *I. Chronicles xxviii. 2*, we are informed "Then David gave to Solomon his son the pattern of the porch, and of the houses thereof." The Hebrew word translated in the Bible as "pattern" also includes "model," and after David had fully explained to Solomon all the details of the intended Temple, we are told, *I. Chronicles xxviii. 20*, "He said to Solomon his son, Be strong and of good courage, and do it."

The first step necessary to be taken in order to put this command into force, was to summon a meeting of the masters of the various trade guilds, at the "Guilds' Hall," so that they could each

EXAMINE THE MODEL,

take out quantities, and ascertain exactly how much of the work would have to be prepared and carried out by their respective guilds.

At the time when King Solomon constructed his Temple he had a number of trade guilds working for him, for instance—

The model or pattern makers' guild.

The gold-smiths guild, which carried out the gold work recorded in *I. Chronicles xxviii. 14*.

The white-smiths, who worked in silver.

The red-smiths, who worked in copper and bronze.

The yellow-smiths, who worked in brass, and who cast the two pillars.

The black-smiths, who worked in iron and steel, and who also had to make and repair all the tools of iron or steel used by the other guilds.

The plumb-smiths worked in lead.

The masons carried out all the stone-work.

The carpenters made the wood-work, and they also constructed the stanchions and levers used in the apparatus for lifting enormous blocks of stone.

The gravers performed any manner of "graving" or carving.

Thus it will be seen that the examination of the "model" furnished each trade with the exact details of the part which it would have to construct and supply in order to make the complete Temple of King Solomon perfect in all its parts and honourable to the trade guilds.

Having now dealt at length with the general system of the trade guild method of working, we will direct our attention to one in particular, namely that of

THE ANCIENT OPERATIVE GUILD OF FREE MASONS.

The question immediately arises, What is Ancient Operative Guild, or Company, Free Masonry? and the official reply is: "The practice of the craft of tectonic art— the science of building temples, important structures, and working in stone in accordance with the ancient usages and established customs of the guild or company."

Naturally, the next question is, When and where were the guilds first established?

We are unable to trace the Ancient Operative guild or craft of Free Mason to its source, or to ascertain the name of the expert master who first devised the complete system of placing the officials and workmen in grades or degrees, by means of which every part of the work was properly and efficiently performed. However, we do know that one of the very earliest and most important steps taken by the founders of the Operative Masons was to divide the work— and consequently the workmen—into two distinct classes, namely,

SQUARE MASONS AND ARCH MASONS,

the reason for this being that the art of performing straight and square work required less skill, and was worth less wages, than the art of making arches, bridges, and all kinds of curved, carved, or graved work.

The investigations which have been made at Babylon prove that the "marks" of both the "Square" and the "Arch" Guild Masons are to be found on the ancient stones, especially is this the case at the "Hanging Gardens."

These gardens were of square form, and in terraces one above another, until they rose as high as the city walls, the whole structure being constructed upon vast arches, raised upon other arches, the top being covered with flat flag-stones upon which was a sheet of lead, upon which was placed the mould for the gardens.

The King of Babylon also instructed his "Square Masons" to prepare stones for "stone roads." These stone roads consisted of two continuous lines of blocks of stone, each being from two feet to six feet in length, one foot in width and about six inches in depth, the distance between the two lines being four feet, and the outside width six feet; consequently it will be seen that the centre or wheel gauge was five feet between the centres.

TECTONIC ART

Railway engineers will not fail to notice that this is practically the gauge of our railways of to-day.

In the traditional history of the early guild masons it is recorded that, "at the making of the tower of Babylon was masons first made much of; and the King of Babylon, called Nimrod, who was a mason himself, loved well the craft And when the city of Nineveh and other cities in the East were to be built, Nimrod sent thither sixty masons at the request of the King of Nineveh his cousin."

"These masons were well cared for and received good pay, the King of Nineveh becoming one of the three Grand Master Masons in his kingdom."

Investigations which were made in Nineveh a few years ago proved that the "Square" and the "Arch" Masons' "marks" were clearly to be seen in the arched vaults and on other stone structures discovered amongst the ruins of that city, and that the "stone roads" were in a good state of preservation.

Some of the Egyptian Masons' Guilds still working at the present time claim and are able to prove that their ancestors have existed more than 5,000 years, and that they originally obtained the craft or "trade secrets" of the operative Free Masons from Atlantis, the lost continent, which once existed to the south-west of Spain, and which is now under the sea, owing of course to an alteration or depression of the crust of the earth.

On the other hand some of the other Egyptian Masons' Guilds have in their possession ancient stone tablets, written in the language of Babylonia, which prove beyond doubt that the King of Babylon sent masons from Babylon to Egypt to instruct the King of Egypt in tectonic art and to form Masons' Trade Guilds in the laud of the Pharoahs.

In Egypt there are also very ancient guilds which have records to prove that their ancestors were employed in the construction of the Pyramids, and they are in possession of the important fact that when a King of Egypt ordered Pyramids to be built it was found by their experts that it would be impossible to work and measure from one side, and consequently it was resolved to "set out" the foundation on the ground by a new "centre" system, in which all the measurements were taken from a centre and a centre plumb line. This method was known as the five point system, because it included the point in the centre, and also each of those at the four corners, and when completed the apex or top of the pyramid formed the fifth point.

There are at the present time Operative Free Masons Building Guilds in China, India, Persia, and the east, which prove by their records, ritual, manners, and customs that they have existed for fully 5,000 years.

The Hebrew Masons' Guilds, one of which went down into Egypt with Jeremiah to Memphis and Assuan, agree with the Guilds of the Egyptians that King Solomon was made a member of the Guild or Craft of Free Mason by King Pharoah, who was at that time the Grand Master Mason of Egypt, and that Solomon paid a very large sum of money to obtain the Guild "trade secrets" and system of building temples.

Operative Masons' Guilds existed in Rome, and there is no doubt that in the year 55, when the Romans came over to Britain, they brought with them from Rome a very large number of Free Masons, and they were at once set to work to build forts, city walls, bridges, and to true up the stones for the great Roman roads.

Immediately after the Romans arrived in England they set to work to make "stone roads" similar to those at Babylon (for instance, the Watling-street and the Foss are well known), in order that their war chariots could keep up a constant communication between the various military camps or centres.

It is an interesting fact that these "stone roads" or "tracks" are found in Egypt. Pompeii and Rome, also that near Weedon, Northamptonshire, at the present day some of the Roman stone road is still in use in the Watling-street.

The Roman Masons were of course formed into Lodges or Guilds, and one of the earliest Free Masons' Guilds in the centre of England was formed near Ullesthorpe at the point at which the Watling-street and Foss-roads cross each other.

Here, 1854 years ago, the Roman General Ostorius Scapula, ordered the Masons to construct a "fort," a "walled camp," and some good private houses. From this point he made an attack upon Leicester, and took it from the Britons, and Free Masons then had Operative Lodges in Leicester, engaged upon the building of city walls, forts, gates, temples, and private houses.

When the Normans came over to England 843 years ago they also brought over a large number of Free Masons.

Guild Masons who were Romans, Danes, Jews, or Normans soon worked together on friendly terms, as they all carried out the Masonic system which they had all originally obtained from Jerusalem and the Grand Lodge of King Solomon.

The Guilds and Companies thus brought to this country have existed ever since, some of the very oldest being in London, York, Berwick, Lancaster, Bristol, Holyhead, and at the Dalkey Hills, near Kingstown, Ireland.

From these details it will be evident that the Guild method of building was a professional architectural "institution," "guild," or "company," having for its object the working in stone and the construction of temples, public buildings, and other stone structures.

To clearly grasp the methods adopted by the "Square" and the "Arch" Masons respectively, it is necessary to consider the two grades separately. We will therefore first take

THE SQUARE MASONS.

The "square masons," who were distinguished by the colour blue, were divided into seven degrees, which commenced with the pupil or apprentice who served for a period of Seven years, in order to become a Free Man, and the seventh being the degree of the Grand Master Mason. The Square Mason used square building stone only, all his work was square, oblong, straight, level, and upright, and by his rules he was not allowed on any account to do any curved, circular, arch, or other form of "round work;" nor might he touch a pair of compasses. He was a "square mason" pure and simple, and his rank was clearly shown by the "blue" devices upon his apron, and by the blue garter, the blue armlet on his right wrist, and the blue badge upon the left breast of his tunic.

It will now be interesting to consider the plan of the ancient "Square" stone-yards at Jerusalem.

There were three stone-yards in a row, with double doors between each, namely, numbers 1, 2, 3 degrees, also three offices, numbers 5, 6, 7, and in addition, there was the site of the Temple or 4th degree.

The "Square" branch of the Ancient Operative Guild, for instance in the days of King Solomon, was divided into seven degrees or grades corresponding to the seven stone-yards and offices.

Seventh Degree.—At the top of the tree the system was controlled by the three Grand Master Masons who had supreme command of the guild. Their office or degree was situated at the western end of the No. 6 degree, and from this seventh office the whole system was ruled and managed, and into this important room no man below "seventh degree rank" might on any account enter.

Sixth Degree.—Next came the experts of the sixth degree rank, mentioned (*I. Kings v. 16*) as "the chief of Solomon's officers which were over the work." They were known as "Passed Masters" because they had successfully passed the examination for a Master. They had to take command of certain departments, also to lay schemes, draw plans, and be responsible to the Grand Masters.

Fifth Degree.—The members of this grade consisted of the "Super-Intendent of works" and (*I. Kings v. 16*) the "three thousand and three hundred, which ruled over the people that wrought in the work" The department being under the Super-Intendent of the Works and his Intendents. This officer had control over the workmen ho appointed new men, discharged men, and heard any complaints that the Task-masters might make against any bad workman, or won't-work," and he decided on the punishment. Thus it will be seen that the first three grades may be said to be practically Masters, Officials, Inspectors, Foreman, and Gangers.

FOURTH DEGREE.

This was the actual site of the building, where the erectors and setters built up the structure.

Every stone had been completed and marked, the reason being that when Solomon laid the first stone of the Temple he made the whole site on Mount Moriah (*II. Chronicles iii. 1*) holy ground. Every man, therefore, employed on the site of the Temple, or 4th degree, be he the Master of Works, Clerk of Works, Erector, or Super-Fellow, had, according to Hebrew custom, to remove his shoes, and keep his head covered, and that is why (*I. Kings vi., 7*) "neither hammer nor axe nor any tool of iron was heard in the house while it was in building."

The men engaged upon the holy work were not allowed to speak, except when necessary to perform their duties, and the Chaplain performed a service daily, at morning, noon, and evening, during the whole seven years that the work was in progress.

It was also in the fourth degree that (*I. Kings v. 17*) "the King commanded, and they brought the great stones" to lay the foundation of the house. It was at the north-east corner of the Temple that the great corner footing-stone was laid. Here also the "foundation sacrifice" was offered, and this accounts for the skeletons which are always found under the corners of the temples and towers both in the East and in some parts of Europe. Why the ancients believed that a building would not last unless a "foundation sacrifice" were offered it is difficult to understand, but such was their belief.

Third Degree.—The third degree "stone-yard" was the place in which all" the "fitting" was done by very expert "Super-Fellows." Here every stone (*I. Kings vi. 7*) was "made ready before it was brought" to the site of the Temple. So that in the "3rd degree yard" the most important fitting had to be done, and every stone was very carefully "marked" by most expert men in the art of marking, so that the actual erectors should have no trouble in putting all the stones properly in their intended places.

Second Degree.—The "Fellows" of the craft in their 2nd stoneyard smoothed and polished the stones to exact gauges, so that every one was true and "up to standard." Every bit of work was tested by a most expert Mason, and anything not up to "sample" was rejected and thrown on the scrap-heap; and the man who did rejected work soon found himself rejected, and had to go down into the "grade below." So a bad workman speedily found his "level" with those "threescore and ten thousand that bare burdens, or the four-score hewers." (*I. Kings v. 15*).

First Degree.—The No. 1 stoneyard contained the "Apprentices" and men of small experience; they worked upon the stone as it came from the quarry and got it into a better form for the "Fellows" to begin upon.

"Hewers in the quarry" were regarded as "quarrymen," and the Masons did not recognise them as members of their trade; in fact, they called them "Low Men" or "Cowans," and would not associate with them.

It will now be interesting to consider the work performed of the ancient "Square" stoneyards at Jerusalem.

In No. 1 yard the apprentices and No. 1 masons worked. The No. 2 yard contained the "Fellows of the Craft," who completed the stones, and made them to perfect size and gauge. In No. 3 yard the stones were fitted together by Super Fellows, and marked by the proper Marked Masters and their assistants.

No. 5 Lodge consisted of 3,300 Overseers, Officers, Inspectors of Material, Task Masters, Deacons, Wardens, and (*I. Kings v. 16*) those who "ruled over the people that wrought in the work." This department was under the Super-Intendent of the Works and his Intendents.

No. 6 Lodge was the Passed Masters.

There were fifteen members of this high rank, mentioned (*I. Kings v., 16*) as "the chief of Solomon's officers." At the western end of the No. 6 degree came the office or degree of the three Grand Master Masons, who ruled the whole system in the 7th office or degree, and into which degree no man below seventh degree rank might on any account enter.

The only possible way for a young man to enter into the ancient guild of a "Square" Mason was for him to apply at the office of the Super-Intendent of the Works, and at the same time get not less than seven persons who are members of the order to propose, second, and support the application, and to speak as to his good character and position.

For a period of four weeks his application must be posted up, and read out aloud as the members passed through the door leading to the works. If at the end of that period the report of good conduct was in his favour he was elected as an apprentice, and was instructed to attend on the following Friday, or sixth day of the week, at twelve o'clock at noon, that being the time of the closing of the week's work, and the only time at which new apprentices were received, initiated into the duties of the Square Mason's Trade, and had their names "entered" upon the Guild Apprentice Roll.

Each apprentice was "bound" both by indentures and by oath, to well and truly serve as a "Mason's Entered Apprentice" for a full term of seven years. It is hardly necessary to mention that during the time he thus served under this "bond" he was not a Free Man or a Free Mason, for the simple reason that he was a "bound man" or "bond man" having to obey orders.

The "Apprenticing ceremony" being completed, the new Brethren were warned to appear at six o'clock a.m. on the first day of the following week, to commence their duties.

On taking their places in the first stone-yard they were each provided with the usual mallet, chisel, and straight-edge, and were set to true up the rough ashlar stone-work from the quarries, and to bring it to about one-sixteenth of an inch larger than the final size required. In other words, they "dressed off the rough," and left the stones right to be "finished" by expert Fellows of the Craft. About a month before the completion of the seven years, the apprentice gave notice to the Super-Intendent of the Works that he should soon be "Free," "out of his bond time," and he applied to be passed as "A Fellow of the Craft."

If the necessary examination proved satisfactory, the man was "accepted" as a Fellow, he became a Free Mason, and a Free Man of the city or town, and was known and addressed as "Fellow." He then, worked in the second degree stone-yard with the "Fellows," not with the apprentices.

After serving for twelve months the Fellow had the right to apply for another rise in position, namely, to be made a Super-Fellow in No. 3 stone-yard. Here he was, employed in fitting all the stones together in their proper positions, and when so fitted, to mark them with the proper Masons' marks so that they could be again placed in Position upon the actual site of the building.

The next advance for a man to make was to the "Fourth Degree" or Erectors; here he would be engaged in the actual erecting and building up of the stones that had been made ready in the three previously-mentioned stone yards. After this experience, the man would apply, and be made an Intendent or Foreman, and hold rank as a "Fifth Degree Man," acting in command of a gang of men and being directly responsible to the Super-Intendent of the Works. The next step was to apply to be examined as a Master. This was a very difficult examination indeed, and required a candidate to know all the practical part of the Mason's profession. If this examination proved satisfactory he was raised to the "Sixth Degree," and ranked as a "Passed Master" of Arts and Sciences. In this position he would remain for many years, as there was only one grade higher that he could attain to, and that was limited to three in number. However, if he was successful and fortunate, he might be selected to be a Grand Master Mason, and thus be one of the three heads who sat in the Office of the Grand Master Masons, or Seventh Degree, who controlled the whole of the Square Guild system of working in tectonic or building art.

As already explained the Square Masons did all the square, level, upright, and straight work, and the Arch Masons carried out all the arch, curved, or circular work. In many instances stones would be required to be square or straight at one end or side, and curved or moulded at the other, and the ancient guild practice was for the stone to be sent from the quarry "rough-hewn" to the square stone yard, where the square work was done in the 1st and 2nd yards, and after being tested and marked in the 3rd yard it was sent to the 1st yard of the Arch Masons so that they could pass it through their 1st, 2nd, and 3rd arch yards, and perform the curved work that was necessary.

THE ARCH MASONS.

The "Arch," round, or "Red" Mason, carried out all kinds of curved stonework; for instance, round columns, arches, pillars, domes, and he also cut skew-backs, voussoirs and key-stones; he used compasses, and measured the circumference of his work and took no notice of diameter. He was not troubled about the ratio 3.14159; his circumference was 1. His circular measure was like our clock faces of to-day, based upon the sexagesimal method in which 60 seconds are a minute, 60 minutes an hour or degree, 30 degrees equal a sign, 90 degrees or three o'clock a quadrant or fourth part of a circle, 360 degrees or twelve hours a complete circle; Thus on one dial they, like ourselves, have time and angles all upon the face of our watches, although we seldom hear a person say "30 degrees one hour," still there is the fact that it is so. The Arch Masons divided their system of working into seven degrees, each held in a circular lodge or stoneyard, the apron, garter, armlet, and badge being "red," and their chief officers are known as the Grand Arch-i-Tectus.

The Arch Masons Guild was divided into seven degrees, and the offices and stone yards were in circles or rings. The inner circle of all was the Seventh Arch-Degree.—Here the three Grand. Arch, Master Masons, or "Arch-i-Tectus," sat and exercised supreme control, and it is important to notice that in the days of Solomon, he and the other two Grand Masters were the heads of both the "Square" arid the "Arch" Masons, so that they had in their own hands the complete control of both classes of work.

Sixth Arch Degree consisted of a ring round the "inner circle." The Passed Arch-i-Tectus here performed the important work, of designing the necessary arch or curved work.

The Fifth Arch Degree was another ring outside the sixth. It was under the control of the "Arch-Superintendent of works," who was assisted by Arch Wardens, Arch Deacons, and Arch Intendents.

The Fourth Arch Degree was a circle upon the site of the building itself, where the arch erectors performed the actual building up of the arched portion of the structure.

The Third Arch Degree was another ring outside the fifth degree, and here all the arch work was tested and marked by the "Arch Markers."

The Second Arch Degree was a ring outside the third in which the work was made to the exact form and dimensions required.

The First Arch Degree was the outer ring of all, in which the "Arch Apprentices" and men of little experience worked.

From the Masters' door at the outside of the outer circle there was a straight walk or "enter-ance" to the centre or inner circle, but as the doors of each circle were carefully guarded by both inner and outer guards, it follows that no person would be able to get through to the inner circle unless he was of the proper rank, and "on business."

Although all the Arch Masons would belong to one or other of the seven degrees, there were also three grades of workmen— (1) The "Arch Mason" who worked in stone for bridges, buildings, and ordinary work. (2) The "Royal Arch Mason" who made arches for the Royal entrance to a building, and also "Arches of Triumph," which were usually constructed of polished granite, and were built after a successful war. (3) The "Holy or Sacred Arch Masons" who only worked in white marble. They constructed the Sacred or Holy Arch which was erected in the Temple of King Solomon, to divide the nave or body of the temple from the chancel and the holy of holies. It is hardly necessary to say that as the Sacred Arch Masons had to erect their work withip the temple, upon holy ground, they wore their hats, removed their shoes from off their feet; and as stated *I. Kings vi. 7*, were not allowed to use "any tool of iron" in the house.

Spon's "Dictionary of Engineering" describes an arch as "a form of structure in which the vertical forces, due to the weight of the material of which it is composed, are transmitted to the supports." However, many thousands of years ago the ancient Guild Masons employed three ways of constructing arches—(1) The ordinary method of "skew-backs," "voussoirs," and a "keystone." (2) The system in which each side of the arch is cut out of one piece of stone or marble, and keyed with a key stone, or three pieces in all. (3) The method of cutting out the whole arch complete so that it could be lifted up into position in one piece.

Arches are found in Babylon, Nineveh, also in Chinese bridges of great antiquity, and investigations prove that in one of the Egyptian pyramids, the "Hawara," there is an arched top to the sarcophagus chamber.

One of the oldest Arch Masons' Guilds in Egypt has in its possession inscriptions on tablets of stone which prove that the science of building stone arches came to them from Babylon.

One authority (Wilkinson) considered that the arched chambers of the Pyramids at Memphis carried the antiquity of the arch back to 2,600 B.C. The stone arch at Saqqara is of the period 600 B.C., and the stone arches of the tombs of Beni Hassan are coeval with Usertensen II. and the Viceroy Joseph.

"Bow" is the name of a very ancient instrument which consisted of a large arch of ninety degrees graduated. From an ancient building guild the writer finds that Bow Church, London, was built by arch stone masons, known as "Companions of the Arch Guild." It was designed by the Master of their Guild and was considered a masterpiece of arch-tect.

The "Treasury of Science" (Maunder) states that the Court of Arches is the Supreme Court belonging to the Archbishop of Canterbury, and that the name originated from the Court having been held in Bow Church, which was built on arches.

Haydn's "Dictionary of Dates," states: — "Arches, Court of, the most ancient consistory court; it derives its name from the Church of St. Mary-le-Bow, London, where it was formally held, and whose top is raised on stone pillars and built archwise."

A "Bow Carpenter" or Centre Maker was a trade to itself, and the members belonged to the Bow Makers' Guild, but worked very closely with the Arch Masons, as their work was to construct the bow or centre of Wood upon which the Arch Mason built his voussoirs, and finally, when he had completed the arch and put in the key stone, the "Bow Carpenter" removed the "centre." As previously mentioned the ancient Arch Masons measured their work by "circumference" "circular" or "round about" measure; for instance, we read *I. Kings vii. 15*, that at the time of Solomon's temple two pillars of brass were cast, "and a line of twelve cubits did compass either of them about." In the *II. Chronicles iv. 2*, we find that a molten sea was cast "and a line of thirty cubits did compass it round about."

The unit of the

ANCIENT HEBREW CIRCULAR MEASURE

was a circle having a circumference of one cubit.

As the royal cubit of Solomon was equal to our English 1,824 foot, it follows that a circle having a diameter of barely 7 inches will give the one circular cubit in circumference, Consequently if we examine a clock face having a diameter of 7 inches we have the Hebrew circular measure. Each minute of time, and each minute of distance, will then be one and the same in length, that is, very similar to our present three-eighths or an inch. Taking 12 o'clock as "0" we then find that 1 o'clock equals 30 degrees; 2, 60; 3, 90; 4, 120 ; 5, 150; 6, 180; 7, 210; 8, 240; 9, 270; 10, 300; 11, 330; 12, 360. It is a very interesting fact that this table of hours and angles has been discovered cut on stone both, in Babylon and in Egypt, and it is preserved by the Arch Masons Guilds in England.

TECTONIC ART

To illustrate the importance of the ancient circular measure the writer by the courtesy of a member of a Masons' Company was able to give a table which related to the English foot. In practice there are many cases in which it is of value to

be able to take the circumference and have the diameter worked out ready, in the same way that the Babylonians did thousands of years ago.

Before closing the details relating to the "Square" and the "Arch" Masons it should be added that two chairs about 250 years old are preserved at the Leicester Corporation Museum, the one has belonged to the Operative Square Guild, and the other to the Arch Guild—both of which guilds met at the White Lion Hotel, Leicester.

SETTING OUT THE CENTRE AND THE CORNERS.

A King or Ruler in ancient times having decided to construct a temple, public building, of pyramid, on a day arranged, attended in state at midday, and at the moment when the sun shone through an aperture fixed in the south, a proper signal was given that it was XII. o'clock noon.

Then with the usual ceremony of the period the "centre stone" was laid by the King, who also with a centre-punch made the centre mark upon the stone, at the same time remarking "There is the centre of the intended structure, work ye to it."

The ancient buildings were usually constructed of one of three forms—(1) Square. (2) Oblong—2 to 1. (3) Oblong 3 to 1.

SQUARE BUILDINGS.

If the building required was to be square, or to have a square-base, as in the case or a pyramid, the King decided upon the size and gave the distance measured from the centre A to each of the four corners F, G, H, I.

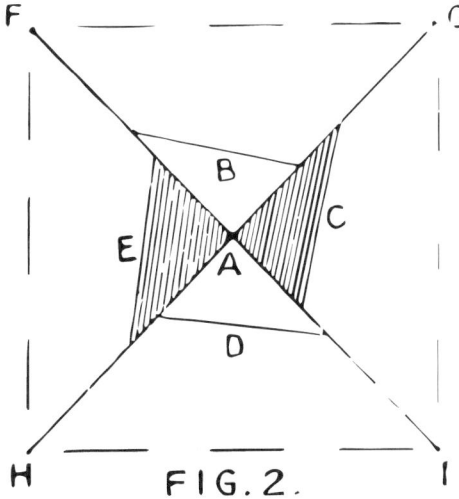

FIG. 2.

14   TECTONIC ART

The length of the sides followed as a matter of course, hut it was not considered in the laying out, which was simply based on the centre and four corner points.

Ancient tradition informs us that "6 times 60 equal to 360 Egyptian cubits was the length of the great pyramid from the centre to the corners, and modern experts estimate the length from the centre as 540 feet, which will give a diameter of 1,080 feet.

The ancient three Master Masons by means of their 3, 4, 5 rods, would then, from the centre struck by the King, form four right angled triangles and place the "pegs" to mark the position of the corners.

As the pegs at the corners would be probably moved or disturbed, the ancient Masons as long ago as the days of Babylon adopted

LANDMARKS.

They saw in those early days that if the pegs at the corners were moved the whole setting out of the work thus far would have to be repeated, therefore they adopted "land-lines" which extended to a considerable distance beyond the actual site of the structure. The land marks were pegs stuck into the ground at such a distance that they would not be disturbed, and it was the duty of every Guild Mason to take great care that these ancient land marks of the order were carefully preserved—in fact in the days of Solomon it was death to move a Free Mason's land mark or land line.

As mentioned previously, the ancients set out the ground plan of their square buildings by the distance from the centre to the four corner's, and they proved the correctness of their work by the "land lines" and "land marks," also they measured the four angles at the centre, each of which of course must in the case of a square building be 90 degrees or the fourth part of a square.

OBLONG BUILDINGS, TWO TO ONE.

In the case of oblong structures built in the proportion of 40 by 20, or two to one, the ancient masons used the same "five point system," but the angle between the diagonal lines at the centre of a building having its length equal to twice its width, is 53.08 degrees as shown. The 53.08 degrees angle of the "3, 4, 5" square being used (A).

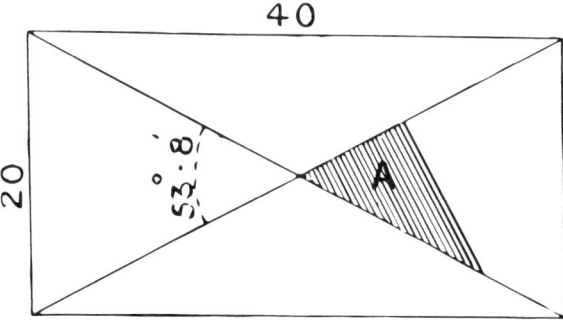

FIG 3

TECTONIC ART 15

OBLONG BUILDINGS, THREE TO ONE.

All ancient temples in all parts of the world were constructed with the main hall or nave three times as long as the width or in the three to one proportion, and the height of the wall was "half the length."

King Solomon's temple was built exactly to this ancient mason's standard, for we read I. Kings vi. 2, "And the house which King Solomon built for the Lord, the length thereof was threescore cubits, the breadth thereof twenty cubits, and the height thereof thirty cubits." This proportion, cut upon stone tablets which have been discovered in Babylon and in Egypt, show that the ancients were fully aware that the angle at the centre formed by a three to one temple is equal to 36 degrees, 52 minutes.

The 36 degrees 52 minutes angle of the Master's square being employed as illustrated (B).

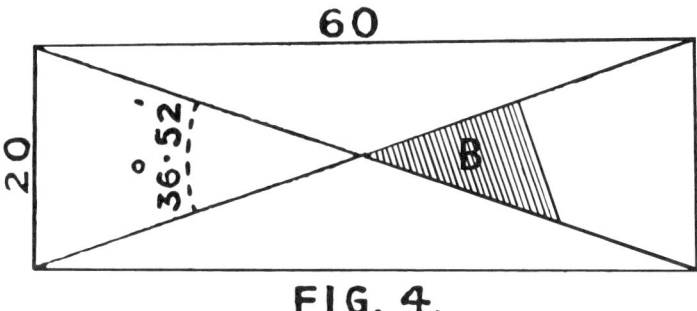

FIG. 4.

It is an interesting fact that many cathedrals and churches in England at the present day have been constructed on the three to one proportion used for temples in Babylon, India, Egypt, and Jerusalem.

The ancient Guild Masons in their records and "traditional history" explain that the reason why they had so much veneration for this proportion, is that the throne of their three Grand Masters had three seats, and rested upon a three to one basis.

From the above illustrations it will be seen that the three angles of the same "Master's square" were used for the laying out of the three forms of building, and it is easy therefore to understand the reason why the building trade secret of laying out on the centre was then preserved by the various "guilds" and "castes."

FOOTING STONES.

In order to give increased bearing surface upon the earth, every building and wall has "wide footings," that is the footing is made considerably wider than the wall or structure which has to rest upon it, and in all the ancient temples and important buildings "footing stones" were used for the foundations. These stones were of great size and weight being in cross section very similar to the letter L back to back.

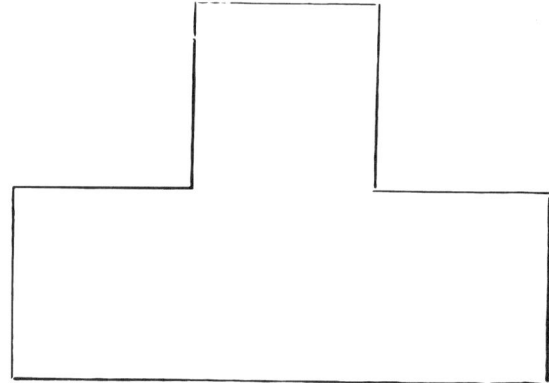

"Footing stones" are well understood by all Installed Masters at the present day, as upon their aprons they have three cross sections of these ancient stones.

The four "corner footing stones" were of similar cross-section but formed the angle at each corner, and those used in the temple of King Solomon were of great size, as the dimensions work out as equal to a weight of no less than 45 tons each.

In the case of very large blocks of stone, such, for instance, as the corner footing stone of a temple, the ancients undermined the huge block of stone in the quarry, so that rollers could be placed under it. Therefore, when the stone was completely cut out it rested upon rollers, and did not have to be lifted. On arrival at the site of the building the stone was rolled on to a stage of timber constructed in the space for the foundation. The stone was then "eased up" sufficiently to enable the stage to be pulled away to the side, and the block was lowered into position. So it will be seen that in the case of "footing stones" there was very little lifting necessary.

THE NORTH EAST CORNER.

It is a well known fact that at the present time, and also for thousands of years past, the first or foundation stone is always laid at the North East corner of the intended structure and the question is frequently asked "Why do you begin at the N.E. any more than at any other corner?"

From the very earliest times, the answer to this question has been carefully preserved as one of the important Trade secrets of Guild Master Masons, but quite recently investigations at Babylon have led to the discovery of inscriptions which give the "reason" in full. As the information has already been made public in Egypt it is no longer a "Trade secret" and the Guilds and Companies of Masons have themselves communicated the following details.

To commence the actual building, the "land lines" must be tightly stretched between the respective "land marks," and at the points of intersection of the four outside "lines," the outside corners of the tops of the four great footing stones must be placed. To place these corners exactly correctly is of the very greatest importance as upon their correctness depends the whole work of erecting. Consequently the best possible light is required to see that the "footing stones" are placed "true to the land lines." The ancient Masons were quite well aware that the best possible light they could have upon the outside of their corner stones was "that great light of heaven," the sun, at the four periods of the day.

THE POSITION OF SOLOMON'S TEMPLE.

The door or "Enter-ance" to the Temple of King Solomon by which the ancients entered, was at the east end of the structure, and the north-east corner footing stone was laid near to the door on the left side of the building, as viewed by a person within the Temple.

THE THRONE IN THE WEST.

The most holy place, the inner courts, the King's throne, and the chancel were all at the west end of the building. The King, the High Priests, and others who were entitled to sit within the sacred chancel-arch, faced the east; but those who only had the right to sit in the nave or body of the Temple faced the west, and worshipped towards the most holy place.

The right or left hand side of the Temple always refers to the right or left of the King as he sat upon his throne in the west and faced the east, and this is made quite clear *II. Chronicles iv, 10* : "And he set the sea on the right side of the east end, over against the south."

In the same way we find that in all the ancient Building Guilds and Masons' Companies, in all parts of the world, the Three Masters are always placed in the west, so that they may see the rising sun in the east. An official is placed in the north to watch the sun at its meridian, and another officer sits in the east, so that he can watch the sun set in the west.

THE FOUNDATION OF THE TEMPLE.

From *II. Chronicles iii.*, also from *I. Kings vi.*, and from the Guild Masons' records, we find that Solomon began to build the temple on Mount Moriah, on the second day of the second month, Zif, which is equal to our month of May, at which time there would be ample sun-light.

At 6 o'clock in the morning Grand Master Mason Solomon began to lay the great North East corner footing stone, because at that time the sun-light was at the outside of the N.E. corner stone. That stone having been "well and truly laid to the land-lines," he proceeded at 10 o'clock to the South East corner and laid the S.E. corner stone as the sun at that time was shining at that corner. After refreshments, he proceeded to the South West corner and there laid the S.W. corner footing stone at 2 o'clock, by which time the sun was shining from the South West, and finally about 5 o'clock he proceeded to the North West corner and laid the N.W. corner stone. Thus it will be seen that the course of the sun was the reason why they commenced the temple at the N.E. corner and worked round to the North West. The four corners being thus "fixed" the work of laying all the inter-mediate "Footing stones" was carried out by Passed Masters or members of the sixth degree.

When the complete oblong foundation of footing stones was in position, the members of the Red Smiths' Guild arrived and placed "double taus of bronze" in the recesses which had been cut for them at the joints of the stones. Then the Plumb-smiths guild, "ran in the taus with melted lead." Thus the foundation was firmly held together, and all visitors to the East at the present day find at Babylon, in Egypt and in Rome the tau marks cut in the ancient stones, but unfortunately most of the bronze taus have been removed.

As soon as the row of footing stones was in position, the ancient Carpenters' Guild erected at the centre and at each corner, "stanchions of wood," and from each of these a plumb-line and plumb-bob was suspended respectively, exactly over the centre which the King had struck, and over the corners. From the centre plumb line the four corners were kept true until the work was completed. It was a well-known maxim that "if they kept true to the centre the corners could not err." It will, of course, be understood that the original centre stone remained in position, and a means was left to get to it in order to ascertain that the work was being carried out "dead upright," and on the "five point system."

Every day the "Super-Intendent" of Works tested the work from the centre, and at twelve o'clock at noon reported to the Grand Masters that "the work is true to the centre."

The ancient Guild Masons were wonderfully particular as to carrying out the work

COURSE BY COURSE.

That is they would not allow any stone of the second course to be laid until the whole of the footing stones were in position, nor might a third course be laid until the second course was completed.

At all the corners the ancients used "corner or angle stones" in the form of a letter L. These were of two sizes known as "long corner" and "short corner," the object being that when built up alternately, "they broke the joint," exactly in the same way that any bricklayer to-day avoids straight joints one over another.

The top row of stones in all ancient temples was formed of head, cope, or capestones, and they were usually twice the size of the ordinary stones.

The Guilds in Jerusalem and in Egypt have an ancient record that when the temple of Solomon was nearly completed and nothing remained but according to ancient custom for the King to lay the great North East "corner-head-stone" that by some error in the "marking" it was sent to the wrong stone-yard on the site of the building, and as it was not wanted there, it was "rejected."

After some delay, the rejected stone was found upon an Arch Guilds' rubbish-heap. The Square Guild Masons soon had it conveyed to its proper place, and thus "the stone which was rejected by the Arch Masons was ultimately laid by Solomon and actually as a fact became the head-stone of the North East corner. The fixing of this head-stone, and also the fixing of the white marble key-stone within the temple, completed the structure ready for the dedication ceremony which is clearly described *I. Kings viii.*

TECTONIC ART

LIFTING STONE.

Frequently we hear the question asked: How did the ancient stone-masons raise the enormous blocks of stone which they used in their temples and pyramids to the heights and positions in which they are now found?

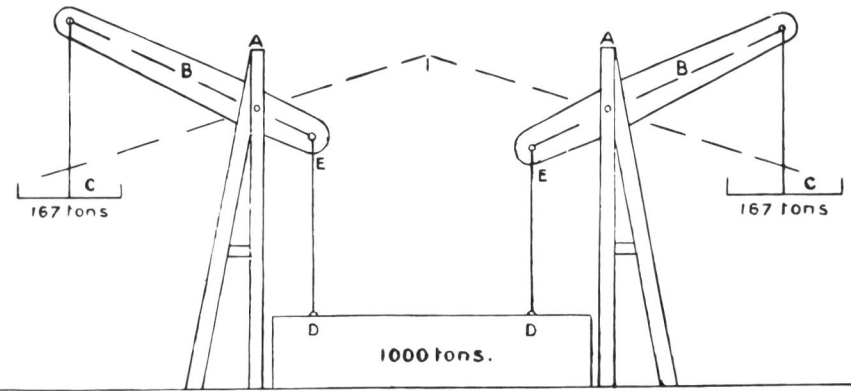

It is a very fortunate fact that the present Guild Masons have full details in China, India, and Egypt which clearly show how the work was carried out. The Carpenters' Guild constructed very strong uprights of timber A, and upon these they placed strong levers B, one end of the lever at E was attached to the stone at D, and the other end was attached to a frame-work upon which weights could be placed—C. To make the system clear we will take two pairs of ordinary scales, of the same size, and place them in a line, with say two feet between them. Place a board of say 2ft. 6in. in length so that the ends rest upon the two inner scales. If the board which represents the weight to be lifted weighs say 2lbs., it follows that if we place a one pound weight in the scale at each end, the "board" will be in perfect "balance." Then half an ounce weight added to or taken from the end scales will either raise or lower the board at our pleasure.

It is a most remarkable fact that this simple matter of "balancing" is fully explained and illustrated on tablets of burnt clay found in Babylon.

If it was necessary to lift a stone of, say, 100 tons, a gang of men was engaged to carry up weights and place them on the frames C, and when 50 tons had been placed at the two ends, of course the stone was in perfect balance, and a few pounds placed on one side or the other would raise or lower the stone as the Master in charge might wish.

If stones of very great weight had to be raised, such for instance, as 1,000 tons, then the levers were made with their outer arms two, three, four, or five times longer than the inner ones. Thus the Ancients obtained enormous power, and with levers of three to one in favour of the power, it follows that 167 tons upon the two end scales at C would lift 1,000 tons in the centre, D.

The stone having been raised a few feet, blocks of wood were placed under it; the levers were returned to the former position, the chains shortened and the process was repeated. Slowly, but surely, the ancient stonemasons lifted great weights to any height by this system. In those days there was unlimited labour and an ample number of men to carry up the necessary weights.

For light lifting they frequently employed the dead weight of men. Twenty men weigh one ton, and 100 men five tons, so if they sent up 100 men to the ends of the two levers it follows that they would raise ten tons without any trouble.

It is very fortunate that the Ancients cut on stone in Egypt, India, and the Holy Land the details of all their methods, so that we, thousands of years later, can clearly see how they carried out their work.

The above details show at a glance that the Ancient Free Masons had a perfect knowledge of levers and balance weights, and they had great knowledge of "wood craft," or they could never have designed the stanchions and balance beams capable of lifting 1.000 tons weight.

If a river or a brook ran near, the Ancients made use of it, and let the water run into tanks, at the end of their levers, and at the sea side, and also in Egypt, they used the rise and fall of the tide. These were known as "the water lifts," and practically are the same as if we place the tray of a pair of scales under a tap of water, for as soon as the dead weight of the water at the one end, exceeded the weight of the load at the other the load must rise, no matter if the load be a pound, a ton, or a thousand tons.

TECTONIC ART

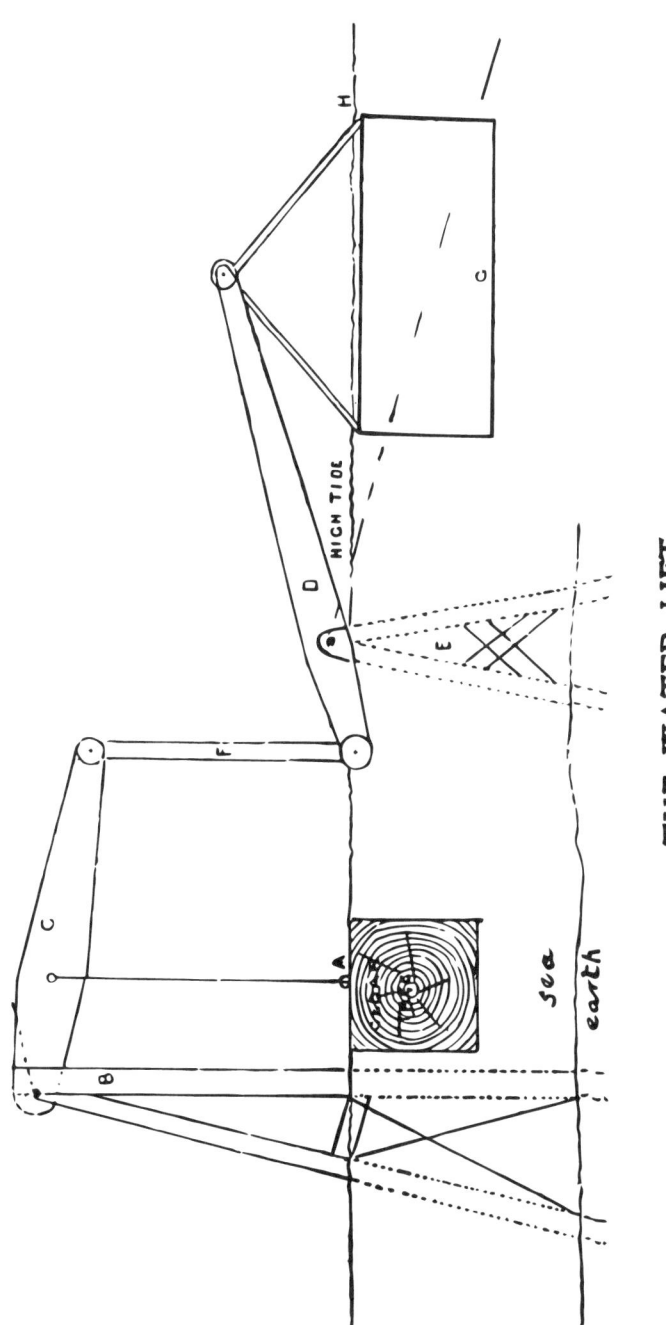

THE WATER LIFT.

THE WATER LIFT.

This form of "lift" was used on the River Nile, also in India, thousands of years ago; also at other sea coasts to raise timber, and was a very simple and mechanical appliance.

At the Egyptian Hall Exhibition of July, 1888, a model was shown of which the annexed diagram is a copy, and a similar model was at the Chicago Exhibition of 1893. A, is the tree to be lifted. B, the staunchion erected in the sea a short distance from the shore. C, a lever of the second order. E, Another staunchion, which carries D, a lever of the first order. F, a connecting-road between the two levers. G, a large tank capable of holding a vast weight of water, and open at the top.

All being ready, the tide rose to H, and the sea filled the tank G. When the tide went down, the tank of water went down, and the cedar tree was raised, and was then supported or "blocked up" until a further lift could be made.

At the conclusion of the first lift, a plug, or door, was opened in the tank, the water was released, and the tank placed again in the position shown. The chain from C to A was shortened, and the process repeated.

If the tide did not rise sufficiently, or the timber was required to be raised quickly, the ancient "Intendent" in charge of the lifting called up a few hundred "carriers of water," and instructed them to carry up water and fill the tank.

In those days there was unlimited labour, and an ample number of men to carry up the necessary weights to the platforms, and when "water lifts" were worked by the rise and fall of the sea it sometimes happened that the work was required to be done quickly, the Task Master would then set a few hundred men to carry buckets of water to place in the tank and provide the lifting power.

As previously mentioned, the Guilds of Free Masons would not include or associate with quarrymen, they looked upon them as "some of those fourscore thousand hewers in the mountains." *I. Kings v. 15*. Free Masons were not allowed to touch a "rough-hewing tool" or 28lb. pointed or "scabbling" hammer. "Cowan" is the name of the man who "rough hewes," and who builds the stone walls between fields in North Wales, Derbyshire, etc., simply by "packing up" rough broken stone. If a Free Mason is asked why he does not include the hewers in his Guild he will reply "My work is stone in courses, Cowan's work is stone out of course." To which the member of the "Hewers' Guild" will generally retort: "Where would you chaps be if we did not hew stone for you."

THE ROUGH HEWERS.

The Hewers Guild in ancient times certainly did some wonderful work, for instance they quarried single blocks of stone which before being "dressed" weighed at least 1,100 tons. To get out such vast blocks they first undermined the stone from one end to the other and then placed rollers under it. Then at the back they cut out some hundreds or square holes, into each of which they dropped down a wedge of wood with the wide end downwards, then they put in a second wedge with the thin end downwards, this system being known as

HEWERS' DOUBLE WEDGING

and was of course one of their trade secrets. Then three powerful men with heavy setting mauls commenced to drive down every one of the uppermost wedges as far as they could, and it was quite usual for 500 or 800 of the strikers to be employed on this work at one time.

Then the "carriers of water" were sent for, and they filled all the holes with water. In time the expansion of the wedges caused the 1,100 ton stone to burst out, and it then rested on the rollers ready tor the "haulers" and some of those "three score and ten thousand that bare burdens" (*1. Kings v. 15*) to come and haul it out of the quarry, and take it to the No. 1 Square Mason's stoneyard for the apprentices to begin upon.

In various parts of the world there are most wonderful examples of

PREHISTORIC GUILD WORK.

One of the most wonderful places is the Indian Madura Temple. There is a door like a tunnel that pierces through a huge pyramid of gods that towers into the sky. Then is reached the temple itself, a silent and echoing city, whose vaulted streets cross one another in all directions, and whose countless people are the stone images graven here. Each column and each monstrous pillar is made of a single block, placed upright by means of the "lifts" previously described, and afterwards deeply sculptured and carved into images of all sorts of gods and monsters. Again, in the grottos of Siva, the god of death, near Golconda, are courts hewn out of the solid granite, and of troops of carved elephants which form the supports of a triple sequence of monolithic temples. Truly a wondrous land, bespeaking a barbaric civilization and splendour at a period when England had hardly come into being. Another perfect piece of prehistoric architecture is the wonderful "mosaic chamber," situated among the famous ruins of the ancient city of Mitla, thirty miles south of the city of Mexico. Although months have been spent by prominent travellers, writers and archaeologists in the attempt to read the history of this old city from the hieroglyphics yet visible on its walls, the only thing known today of Mitla or its buildings, of architecture, of temples and palaces, is grouped on a slight elevation besides a narrow stream. Even the name of Mitla is of unknown origin. But while every structure of which this group is composed is covered within and without with mosaics, it remains for the great Hall known as the "mosaic chamber" to reveal the work at its best. The marvellous part is that there is not a single piece of tile missing from the entire room. These mosaics were put together without the aid of cement or mortar.

Some portion of the ruins of Mitla had been covered with sand for unknown centuries when the Mexican government began excavating, but the larger portion of the buildings were above the ground, exposed to the elements. About two hundred and seventy-five years ago one of the Mitla temples was pulled down, and a church built with the stone. This the natives call the "new church," although it is nearly three hundred years old.

Beneath one of the temples of Mitla an underground chamber has been found, and under this is believed to be another subterranean room, which the Mexican government is now taking steps to investigate. It is fully expected that the old

Guild method of building from a "centre plumb line" will be found in this lower room, and great interest is being taken in the matter.

One of the most sacred shrines of India, which had been for centuries the goal of pilgrimages from all parts of India, was the great temple of Ramesvara, sacred to Rama, situated on an island close to the mainland, in the channel between South India and Ceylon. It had a magnificent Gopuram. Its most striking feature, however, was the wonderful corridors which adorned it. The south corridor was 700ft. in length, that is to say, it was the longest in the world except that in the Vatican. The most attractive of all the Chalukyan shrines was the great temple of Siva at Halebid, about twenty miles from Belun, built on a terrace slanting down to the lake.

In the year 1270 A.D. it was left unfinished, and the towers have never been completed. It was one of the most remarkable monuments in India. One of the pavilions in front contained a huge image of the Bull of Siva. In the interior were some remarkable black stone pillars, which looked as if they had been turned in a lathe. This temple was unmatched in the variety of its details and the exuberance of fancy shown in its ornamentation. There is, perhaps, no other temple in the world on the outside carving of which such a marvellous amount of graving has been performed. It will give some idea of the enormous amount of sculpture with which this temple was covered when it is mentioned that the lowest band of the frieze alone contained a procession of about 2,000 elephants, no two of which are exactly alike.

Now turning to the wonders of Egypt, in one of the caverns at Memphis there are numerous sarcophagi in granite blocks, weighing from 60 to 80 thousand kilos—says a French writer. Mariette Bey endeavoured to get one of the smallest of them removed. But all his efforts only enabled him to draw the monolith a little further towards the passage.

Over the top of the door of Solomon's temple there was placed a very long and large "head-stone" or lintel. It contained no less than 60 cube cubits of stone, and was regarded as the height of Square Mason's tectonic Art.

This stone, which was placed in position by the King, had "graved" upon it in Hebrew characters, the first Words of that Holy Book:

"IN THE BEGINNING GOD CREATED

THE HEAVEN AND THE EARTH."

The letters themselves were of solid gold, and let into the graved part of the stone. It was, therefore, indeed, a work of art worthy of the King, the nation, the masons, and the goldsmiths' guild.

After investigations one can only come to the conclusion that years ago in the Guild days there were some wonderfully clever men engaged in the ancient system.

TECTONIC ART

In England, St. Paul's Cathedral was commenced in the year 1675, by the St. Paul's Guild of Free Masons, the stone being made ready at Portland and sent to London by water.

THE GUILDS IN ENGLAND DECLINE.

In 1710 the Rev. James Anderson was the Chaplain of the St. Paul's Guild Masons, who, at that time, had their head quarters at the Goose and Gridiron Alehouse in St. Paul's churchyard. London, and in September, 1714, the books of the Guild shew that Anderson had made a very remarkable "innovation" in the rules, which was, to admit persons as members of the Masons' Guild without their serving the seven years' apprenticeship. This caused a split in the ranks. Many of the Masters and Passed Masters of the Guilds in various parts of the country joined the new system of Dr. Anderson.

At the White Lion Hotel, Leicester, for instance, a Guild had existed for a very long period, but in 1790 the chief members became members of the system of Anderson, termed by the Guilds "Andersonry." At a later date the workmen of the lower grades all decided that they would not continue to work under the Guild system, and no boys would serve the seven years' apprenticeship.

Soon after the Trade Union Act of 1871 was passed, the new "Stonemasons' Trade Union," took over as members a large majority of the Guild members, and at the present time although Masons' Companies and Guilds exist in England the writer is not aware that any stone-yard since 1883 has been managed and controlled upon the ancient Guild system of the Free Masons.

In conclusion the writer may say that for thousands of years guilds have carried out the most strict letter of the law not to allow outsiders to obtain the very "least trace" of the ancient systems; but now several of them have decided that it is perfectly lawful to have the "bare facts" of their history written by their own respective officials. It must therefore be understood that the recent articles in the Melton Times are not by any means the complete history, but only so much as the writer has received authority to make known to the readers.

Author's Note.

For thousands of years Guilds in general and the Free Masons' Guild in particular, carried out the most strict letter of the law, not to allow outsiders to obtain the very "least trace" of the Ancient system of working, but a few years ago at a meeting held at York it was decided that it was perfectly lawful to give certain "bare facts" on condition that the proposed article or communication be first sent to the proper Officer for his "mark of approval."

During the past few years a number of interesting visits, have been paid to quarries, Iron works, Coal mines and Engineering works in or near Leicestershire, and at several of the quarries much interest was taken in the fact that although the work was not being carried out under the Guild system, many of the workmen "proved themselves by proper signs" to be members of the Ancient Operative Masons' Guild, which system has come down to us from Babylon.

When the writer was first asked to draw up a paper on Operative Masonry he feared that it would be impossible to write anything of interest without running the risk of saying too much. However, after consultation with a Grand Master Mason the work was undertaken.

When the M.S. was completed it was duly forwarded to the proper Officer, and came back with the necessary "mark of approval" and very highly commended, as "the best thing that had been written upon this subject."

On the 20th, February last the paper was read before the Leicester Association of Engineers, at their meeting held at the Technical School, Leicester, and the reports of the same have appeared in the "Melton Mowbray Times" for March 12th and 26th, April 2nd, 9th and 16th.

Naturally it is pleasing to the writer to find that the articles have proved of so much public interest that they are to be reproduced in the present pamphlet form.

Saxe Coburg House,　　　　　　　　CLEMENT E. STRETTON,
　Leicester, April 19th, 1909.　　　　　　　　(Masons' Guild, 7th degree).

TECTONIC ART.

Ancient Trade Guilds and Companies.

Free Masons' Guilds.

By CLEMENT E. STRETTON.

TRADE Guilds, Castes, Societies, Companies and similar institutions have existed from a very remote but unknown period in the world's history, and a reference to Whitaker's Almanack will show that in London alone there are fully eighty of these ancient trade companies still in existence at the present day.

The Lord Mayor of London is always selected from the members of one or other of these City Livery Companies, and it is a well-known fact that a copy of every book printed in this country, for sale, has by law to be forwarded to the Stationers' Company at their Stationers' Hall, London.

The origin of all the trade guilds, many thousands of years ago, was the desire of each trade to keep its particular art, science, knowledge, method, system or craft in its own hands, in other words to strictly preserve the respective "trade secrets."

Experts who have made investigations amongst the ruins of Babylon have been able to obtain proof from the ancient inscriptions and marks, that the Guild system for all trades was in use at the time when that city was built, also that the King of Babylon, Nimrod, was either a Grand Master or a Protector of every trade guild.

All the guilds which work in metal, in all parts of the world, in their "Traditional History" state that
"Tubal-Cain founded the smith-craft of
"gold, silver, iron, copper, bronze,
"steel, and other metals."

The Building Guilds have records that
"Jabal founded the craft of geometry,
"and first wrought houses of stone."

The Weavers' Guilds claim that
"Naamah founded the craft of weaving."

The Musicians' Guild states that
"Jubal was the father of all such as
"handle the harp and the organ, and
"the craft of music and song of mouth."

To carry out its system each trade guild divided its methods and also its members into grades or degrees, and the officers and workmen were instructed in that particular portion of the art or craft which belonged to the respective degree of which they were members, consequently it will be evident that to obtain the full knowledge of any trade a person must begin as an apprentice in the lowest grade and by skill and attention to duty, gradually "work up" to be a Master or chief ruler of his Guild.

The number of grades or degrees varied according to the practical requirements of the trade, but in each instance it follows that if a young man desired to work in any of the trades he must belong to the Trade Guild, as the members would neither teach nor work with any "outsider." The young man must seek and find the respective Trades Hall and make formal application to be made an apprentice to the trade, and bring at least seven persons who must satisfy a master or other officials as to his good character; also that he has not previously been an apprentice to any other guild, and that he has never been discharged or expelled the work without authority. His application having in due time been received and accepted he attended at the proper time to go through the formal ceremony of being "apprenticed."

The "proper time" in every case was twelve o'clock at noon on the last day of the week, that being the only time when "apprentices" were "made." Every guild required the candidate to "Fear God, honour the King, obey the ancient charges, and strictly preserve the secrets of the trade."

Having been sworn, and "charged," his name was entered upon the roll of apprentices. He was then provided with the proper working tools used in the trade, being carefully taught and instructed how to use them. He was always addressed as Brother, and officially described as "an entered apprentice to the craft of—" (in accordance with the name of the trade).

After the "Day of Rest" the apprentice commenced regular work, being placed with the other new hands in the lowest room, yard, or degree, where they were all under the special control of expert members of the craft or calling.

Gradually the young apprentice progressed, and was promoted to higher work and rank in exact accordance with his skill, knowledge and ability, and in time it was open to him to attain to the highest office in his guild.

"Efficiency"—the power, skill, knowledge and will to perform the allotted task, whatever it might be, in a proper workmanlike manner, was the object and desire of every guild member; therefore, to say that a person was a master of his craft was an honour to him.

The particulars above given show the general outline which applied, and still applies, to all the ancient guilds in all parts of the world, and attention must now be directed to

THE GUILD SYSTEM OF WORKING.

In the construction of any building of importance it follows that the members of many guilds must be employed, and consequently it is of very great importance that the chief officers of each guild should be perfectly well acquainted with the particular portion of the work which each has to perform and carry out.

As an instance, let it be assumed that a very important building be required, such as a temple at Jerusalem.

The first step towards the erection of such an edifice was to decide upon the "unit of measure" to be adopted, and, secondly, to have a complete model constructed to scale, showing every part of the building and its fittings made in the proper material. In ancient times each nation had two standard units of measure. The one was the unit for ordinary use and for civil purposes, the other was the Royal measure, used for ecclesiastical buildings, temples, kings' palaces, and the most important structures.

For instance the Hebrews at Jerusalem had a short cubit for general use based upon the length of a man's arm from the elbow to the tip of the middle finger, or very nearly equal to our modern 18 inches. They also had a Royal cubit which is clearly explained by Ezekiel xl. 5, who shows that the Royal or long cubit was a short "cubit and an hand breadth," therefore it follows that the Royal cubit was equal to our 1.824 English foot, or very similar to the present 21 7-8th inches.

This long cubit was divided into 60 minutes in length, each being very similar to our 3-8ths of an inch, each minute being again divided into 60 parts known as seconds.

If we refer to the volume of the S.L. II. Chronicles iii. 3, it will be found that King David instructed Solomon when building the temple to adopt "The length by cubits after the first measure." The word here translated in the English Bible as "first" should read "first importance" or the Royal measure.

In I. Chronicles xxviii. 2, we are informed "Then David gave to Solomon his son the *pattern* of the porch, and of the houses thereof." The Hebrew word translated in the Bible as "pattern" also includes "model," and after David had fully explained to Solomon all the details of the intended Temple, we are told, I. Chronicles xxviii. 20, "He said to Solomon his son, Be strong and of good courage, and do it."

The first step necessary to be taken in order to put this command into force, was to summon a meeting of the masters of the various trade guilds, at the "Guilds' Hall," so that they could each

EXAMINE THE MODEL,

take out quantities, and ascertain exactly how much of the work would have to be prepared and carried out by their respective guilds.

At the time when King Solomon constructed his Temple he had a number of trade guilds working for him, for instance—

The model or pattern makers' guild.

The gold-smiths guild, which carried out the gold work recorded in I. Chronicles xxviii. 14.

The white-smiths, who worked in silver.

The red-smiths, who worked in copper and bronze.

The yellow-smiths, who worked in brass, and who cast the two pillars.

The black-smiths, who worked in iron and steel, and who also had to make and repair all the tools of iron or steel used by the other guilds.

The plumb-smiths worked in lead.

The masons carried out all the stone-work.

The carpenters made the wood-work, and they also constructed the stanchions and levers used in the apparatus for lifting enormous blocks of stone.

The gravers performed any manner of "graving" or carving.

Thus it will be seen that the examination of the "model" furnished each trade with the exact details of the part which it would have to construct and supply in order to make the complete Temple of King Solomon perfect in all its parts and honourable to the trade guilds.

Having now dealt at length with the general system of the trade guild method of working, we will direct our attention to one in particular, namely that of

THE ANCIENT OPERATIVE GUILD OF FREE MASONS.

The question immediately arises, What is Ancient Operative Guild, or Company, Free Masonry? and the official reply is: "The practice of the craft of tectonic art— the science of building temples, important structures, and working in stone in accordance with the ancient usages and established customs of the guild or company."

Naturally, the next question is, When and where were the guilds first established?

We are unable to trace the Ancient Operative guild or craft of Free Mason to its source, or to ascertain the name of the expert master who first devised the complete system of placing the officials and workmen in grades or degrees, by means of which every part of the work was properly and efficiently performed. However, we do know that one of the very earliest and most important steps taken by the founders of the Operative Masons was to divide the work— and consequently the workmen—into two distinct classes, namely,

SQUARE MASONS AND ARCH MASONS,

the reason for this being that the art of performing straight and square work required less skill, and was worth less wages, than the art of making arches, bridges, and all kinds of curved, carved, or graved work.

The investigations which have been made at Babylon prove that the "marks" of both the "Square" and the "Arch" Guild Masons are to be found on the ancient stones, especially is this the case at the "Hanging Gardens."

These gardens were of square form, and in terraces one above another, until they rose as high as the city walls, the whole structure being constructed upon vast arches, raised upon other arches, the top being covered with flat flag-stones upon which was a sheet of lead, upon which was placed the mould for the gardens.

The King of Babylon also instructed his "Square Masons" to prepare stones for "stone roads." These stone roads consisted of two continuous lines of blocks of stone, each being from two feet to six feet in length, one foot in width and about six inches in depth, the distance between the two lines being four feet, and the outside width six feet; consequently it will be seen that the centre or wheel gauge was five feet between the centres.

Railway engineers will not fail to notice that this is practically the gauge of our railways of to-day.

In the traditional history of the early guild masons it is recorded that, "at the making of the tower of Babylon was masons first made much of; and the King of Babylon, called Nimrod, who was a mason himself, loved well the craft. And when the city of Nineveh and other cities in the East were to be built, Nimrod sent thither sixty masons at the request of the King of Nineveh his cousin."

"These masons were well cared for and received good pay, the King of Nineveh becoming one of the three Grand Master Masons in his kingdom."

Investigations which were made in Nineveh a few years ago proved that the "Square" and the "Arch" Masons' "marks" were clearly to be seen in the arched vaults and on other stone structures discovered amongst the ruins of that city, and that the "stone roads" were in a good state of preservation.

Some of the Egyptian Masons' Guilds still working at the present time claim and are able to prove that their ancestors have existed more than 5,000 years, and that they originally obtained the craft or "trade secrets" of the operative Free Masons from Atlantis, the lost continent, which once existed to the south-west of Spain, and which is now under the sea, owing of course to an alteration or depression of the crust of the earth.

On the other hand some of the other Egyptian Masons' Guilds have in their possession ancient stone tablets, written in the language of Babylonia, which prove beyond doubt that the King of Babylon sent masons from Babylon to Egypt to instruct the King of Egypt in tectonic art and to form Masons' Trade Guilds in the land of the Pharoahs.

In Egypt there are also very ancient guilds which have records to prove that their ancestors were employed in the construction of the Pyramids, and they are in possession of the important fact that when a King of Egypt ordered Pyramids to be built it was found by their experts that it would be impossible to work and measure from one side, and consequently it was resolved to "set out" the foundation on the ground by a new "centre" system, in which all the measurements were taken from a centre and a centre plumb line. This method was known as the five point system, because it included the point in the centre, and also each of those at the four corners, and when completed the apex or top of the pyramid formed the fifth point.

There are at the present time Operative Free Masons Building Guilds in China, India, Persia, and the east, which prove by their records, ritual, manners, and customs that they have existed for fully 5,000 years.

The Hebrew Masons' Guilds, one of which went down into Egypt with Jeremiah to Memphis and Assuan, agree with the Guilds of the Egyptians that King Solomon was made a member of the Guild or Craft of Free Mason by King Pharoah, who was at that time the Grand Master Mason of Egypt, and that Solomon paid a very large sum of money to obtain the Guild "trade secrets" and system of building temples.

Operative Masons' Guilds existed in Rome, and there is no doubt that in the year 55, when the Romans came over to Britain, they brought with them from Rome a very large number of Free Masons, and they were at once set to work to build forts, city walls, bridges, and to true up the stones for the great Roman roads.

Immediately after the Romans arrived in England they set to work to make "stone roads" similar to those at Babylon (for instance, the Watling-street and the Foss are well known), in order that their war chariots could keep up a constant communication between the various military camps or centres.

It is an interesting fact that these "stone roads" or "tracks" are found in Egypt, Pompeii and Rome, also that near Weedon, Northamptonshire, at the present day some of the Roman stone road is still in use in the Watling-street.

The Roman Masons were of course formed into Lodges or Guilds, and one of the earliest Free Masons' Guilds in the centre of England was formed near Ulleshorpe at the point at which the Watling-street and Foss-roads cross each other.

Here, 1854 years ago, the Roman General Ostorius Scapula, ordered the Masons to construct a "fort," a "walled camp," and some good private houses. From this point he made an attack upon Leicester, and took it from the Britons, and Free Masons then had Operative Lodges in Leicester, engaged upon the building of city walls, forts, gates, temples, and private houses.

When the Normans came over to England 843 years ago they also brought over a large number of Free Masons.

Guild Masons who were Romans, Danes, Jews, or Normans soon worked together on friendly terms, as they all carried out the Masonic system which they had all originally obtained from Jerusalem and the Grand Lodge of King Solomon.

The Guilds and Companies thus brought to this country have existed ever since, some of the very oldest being in London, York, Berwick, Lancaster, Bristol, Holyhead, and at the Dalkey Hills, near Kingstown, Ireland.

From these details it will be evident that the Guild method of building was a professional architectural "institution," "guild," or "company," having for its object the working in stone and the construction of temples, public buildings, and other stone structures.

To clearly grasp the methods adopted by the "Square" and the "Arch" Masons respectively, it is necessary to consider the two grades separately. We will therefore first take

THE SQUARE MASONS.

The "square masons," who were distinguished by the colour blue, were divided into seven degrees, which commenced with the pupil or apprentice who served for a period of Seven years, in order to become a Free Man, and the seventh being the degree of the Grand Master Mason. The Square Mason used square building stone only, all his work was square, oblong, straight, level, and upright, and by his rules he was not allowed on any account to do any curved, circular, arch, or other form of "round work;" nor might he touch a pair of compasses. He was a "square mason" pure and simple, and his rank was clearly shown by the "blue" devices upon his apron, and by the blue garter, the blue armlet on his right wrist, and the blue badge upon the left breast of his tunic.

It will now be interesting to consider the plan of the ancient "Square" stoneyards at Jerusalem.

There were three stone-yards in a row, with double doors between each, namely, numbers 1, 2, 3 degrees, also three offices, numbers 5, 6, 7, and, in addition, there was the site of the Temple or 4th degree.

The "Square" branch of the Ancient Operative Guild, for instance in the days of King Solomon, was divided into seven degrees or grades corresponding to the seven stone-yards and offices.

Seventh Degree.—At the top of the tree the system was controlled by the three Grand Master Masons who had supreme command of the guild. Their office or degree was situated at the western end of the No. 6 degree, and from this seventh office the whole system was ruled and managed, and into this important room no man below "seventh degree rank" might on any account enter.

Sixth Degree.—Next came the experts of the sixth degree rank, mentioned (I. Kings v. 16) as "the chief of Solomon's officers which were over the work." They were known as "Passed Masters" because they had successfully passed the examination for a Master. They had to take command of certain departments, also to lay schemes, draw plans, and be responsible to the Grand Masters.

Fifth Degree.—The members of this grade consisted of the "Super-Intendent of works," and (I. Kings v. 16) the "three thousand and three hundred, which ruled over the people that wrought in the work" The department being under the Super-Intendent of the Works and his Intendents. This officer had control over the workmen, he appointed new men, discharged men, and heard any complaints that the Task-masters might make against any bad workman, or "won't-work," and he decided on the punishment. Thus it will be seen that the first three grades may be said to be practically Masters, Officials, Inspectors, Foreman, and Gangers.

FOURTH DEGREE.

This was the actual site of the building, where the erectors and setters built up the structure.

Every stone had been completed and marked, the reason being that when Solomon laid the first stone of the Temple he made the whole site on Mount Moriah (II. Chronicles iii. 1) holy ground. Every man, therefore, employed on the site of the Temple, or 4th degree, be he the Master of Works, Clerk of Works, Erector, or Super-Fellow, had, according to Hebrew custom, to remove his shoes, and keep his head covered, and that is why (I. Kings vi., 7) "neither hammer nor axe nor any tool of iron was heard in the house while it was in building."

The men engaged upon the holy work were not allowed to speak, except when necessary to perform their duties, and the Chaplain performed a service daily, at morning, noon, and evening, during the whole seven years that the work was in progress.

It was also in the fourth degree that (I. Kings v. 17) "the King commanded, and they brought the great stones" to lay the foundation of the house. It was at the north-east corner of the Temple that the great corner footing-stone was laid. Here also the "foundation sacrifice" was offered, and this accounts for the skeletons which are always found under the corners of the temples and towers both in the East and in some parts of Europe. Why the ancients believed that a building would not last unless a "foundation sacrifice" were offered it is difficult to understand, but such was their belief.

Third Degree.—The third degree "stoneyard" was the place in which all the "fitting" was done by very expert "Super-Fellows." Here every stone (I. Kings vi. 7) was "made ready before it was brought" to the site of the Temple. So that in the "3rd degree yard" the most important fitting had to be done, and every stone was very carefully "marked" by most expert men in the art of marking, so that the actual erectors should have no trouble in putting all the stones properly in their intended places.

Second Degree.—The "Fellows" of the craft in their 2nd stoneyard smoothed and polished the stones to exact gauges, so that every one was true and "up to standard." Every bit of work was tested by a most expert Mason, and anything not up to "sample" was rejected and thrown on the scrap-heap; and the man who did rejected work soon found himself rejected, and had to go down into the "grade below." So a bad workman speedily found his "level" with those "threescore and ten thousand that bare burdens, or the four-score hewers." (I. Kings v. 15).

First Degree.—The No. 1 stoneyard contained the "Apprentices" and men of small experience; they worked upon the stone as it came from the quarry and got it into a better form for the "Fellows" to begin upon.

"Hewers in the quarry" were regarded as "quarrymen," and the Masons did not recognise them as members of their trade; in fact, they called them "Low Men" or "Cowans," and would not associate with them.

It will now be interesting to consider the work performed of the ancient "Square" stoneyards at Jerusalem.

In No. 1 yard the apprentices and No. 1 masons worked. The No. 2 yard contained the "Fellows of the Craft," who completed the stones, and made them to perfect size and gauge. In No. 3 yard the stones were fitted together by Super Fellows, and marked by the proper Marked Masters and their assistants.

No. 5 Lodge consisted of 3,300 Overseers, Officers, Inspectors of Material, Task Masters, Deacons, Wardens, and (I. Kings v., 16) those who "ruled over the people that wrought in the work." This department was under the Super-Intendent of the Works and his Intendents.

No. 6 Lodge was the Passed Masters.

There were fifteen members of this high rank, mentioned (I. Kings v., 16) as "the chief of Solomon's officers." At the western end of the No. 6 degree came the office or degree of the three Grand Master Masons, who ruled the whole system in the 7th office or degree, and into which degree no man below seventh degree rank might on any account enter.

The only possible way for a young man to enter into the ancient guild of a "Square" Mason was for him to apply at the office of the Super-Intendent of the Works, and at the same time get not less than seven persons who are members of the order to propose, second, and support the application, and to speak as to his good character and position.

For a period of four weeks his application must be posted up, and read out aloud as the members passed through the door leading to the works. If at the end of that period the report of good conduct was in his favour he was elected as an apprentice, and was instructed to attend on the following Friday, or sixth day of the week, at twelve o'clock at noon, that being the time of the closing of the week's work, and the only time at which new apprentices were received, initiated into the duties of the Square Mason's Trade, and had their names "entered" upon the Guild Apprentice Roll.

Each apprentice was "bound" both by indentures and by oath, to well and truly serve as a "Mason's Entered Apprentice" for a full term of seven years. It is hardly necessary to mention that during the time he thus served under this "bond" he was not a Free Man or a Free Mason, for the simple reason that he was a "bound man" or "bond man" having to obey orders.

The "Apprenticing ceremony" being completed, the new Brethren were warned to appear at six o'clock a.m. on the first day of the following week, to commence their duties.

On taking their places in the first stone-yard they were each provided with the usual mallet, chisel, and straight-edge, and were set to true up the rough ashlar stone-work from the quarries, and to bring it to about one-sixteenth of an inch larger than the final size required. In other words, they "dressed off the rough," and left the stones right to be "finished" by expert Fellows of the Craft. About a month before the completion of the seven years, the apprentice gave notice to the Super-Intendent of the Works that he should soon be "Free," "out of his bond time," and he applied to be passed as "A Fellow of the Craft."

If the necessary examination proved satisfactory, the man was "accepted" as a Fellow, he became a Free Mason, and a Free Man of the city or town, and was known and addressed as "Fellow." He then worked in the second degree stone-yard with the "Fellows," not with the apprentices.

After serving for twelve months the Fellow had the right to apply for another rise in position, namely, to be made a Super-Fellow in No. 3 stone-yard. Here he was employed in fitting all the stones together in their proper positions, and when so fitted, to mark them with the proper Masons' marks so that they could be again placed in position upon the actual site of the building.

The next advance for a man to make was to the "Fourth Degree" or Erectors; here he would be engaged in the actual erecting and building up of the stones that had been made ready in the three previously-mentioned stone yards. After this experience, the man would apply, and be made an Intendent or Foreman, and hold rank as a "Fifth Degree Man," acting in command of a gang of men and being directly responsible to the Super-Intendent of the Works. The next step was to apply to be examined as a Master. This was a very difficult examination indeed, and required a candidate to know all the practical part of the Mason's profession. If this examination proved satisfactory he was raised to the "Sixth Degree," and ranked as a "Passed Master" of Arts and Sciences. In this position he would remain for many years, as there was only one grade higher that he could attain to, and that was limited to three in number. However, if he was successful and fortunate, he might be selected to be a Grand Master Mason, and thus be one of the three heads who sat in the Office of the Grand Master Masons, or Seventh Degree, who controlled the whole of the Square Guild system of working in tectonic or building art.

As already explained the Square Masons did all the square, level, upright, and straight work, and the Arch Masons carried out all the arch, curved, or circular work. In many instances stones would be required to be square or straight at one end or side, and curved or moulded at the other, and the ancient guild practice was for the stone to be sent from the quarry "rough-hewn" to the square stone yard, where the square work was done in the 1st and 2nd yards, and after being tested and marked in the 3rd yard it was sent to the 1st yard of the Arch Masons so that they could pass it through their 1st, 2nd, and 3rd arch yards, and perform the curved work that was necessary.

THE ARCH MASONS.

The "Arch," round, or "Red" Mason, carried out all kinds of curved stonework; for instance, round columns, arches, pillars, domes, and he also cut skew-backs, voussoirs, and key-stones; he used compasses, and measured the circumference of his work and took no notice of diameter. He was not troubled about the ratio 3.14159; his circumference was 1. His circular measure was like our clock faces of to-day, based upon the sexagesimal method in which 60 seconds are a minute, 60 minutes an hour or degree, 30 degrees equal a sign, 90 degrees or three o'clock a quadrant or fourth part of a circle, 360 degrees or twelve hours a complete circle. Thus on one dial they, like ourselves, have time and angles all upon the face of our watches, although we seldom hear a person say "30 degrees one hour," still there is the fact that it is so. The Arch Masons divided their system of working into seven degrees, each held in a circular ledge or stoneyard, the apron, garter, armlet, and badge being "red," and their chief officers are known as the Grand Arch-i-Tectus.

The Arch Masons Guild was divided into seven degrees, and the offices and stone yards were in circles or rings. The inner circle of all was the

Seventh Arch Degree.—Here the three Grand Arch Master Masons, or "Arch-i-Tectus," sat and exercised supreme control, and it is important to notice that in the days of Solomon, he and the other two Grand Masters were the heads of both the "Square" and the "Arch" Masons, so that they had in their own hands the complete control of both classes of work.

Sixth Arch Degree consisted of a ring round the "inner circle." The Passed Arch-i-Tectus here performed the important work of designing the necessary arch or curved work.

The Fifth Arch Degree was another ring outside the sixth. It was under the control of the "Arch Superintendent of works," who was assisted by Arch Wardens, Arch Deacons, and Arch Intendents.

The Fourth Arch Degree was a circle upon the site of the building itself, where the arch erectors performed the actual building up of the arched portion of the structure.

The Third Arch Degree was another ring outside the fifth degree, and here all the arch work was tested and marked by the "Arch Markers."

The Second Arch Degree was a ring outside the third in which the work was made to the exact form and dimensions required.

The First Arch Degree was the outer ring of all, in which the "Arch Apprentices" and men of little experience worked.

From the Masters' door at the outside of the outer circle there was a straight walk or "enter-ance" to the centre or inner circle, but as the doors of each circle were carefully guarded by both inner and outer guards, it follows that no person would be able to get through to the inner circle unless he was of the proper rank, and "on business."

Although all the Arch Masons would belong to one or other of the seven degrees, there were also three grades of workmen—(1) The "Arch Mason" who worked in stone for bridges, buildings, and ordinary work. (2) The "Royal Arch Mason" who made arches for the Royal entrance to a building, and also "Arches of Triumph," which were usually constructed of polished granite, and were built after a successful war. (3) The "Holy or Sacred Arch Masons" who only worked in white marble. They constructed the Sacred or Holy Arch which was erected in the Temple of King Solomon, to divide the nave or body of the temple from the chancel and the holy of holies. It is hardly necessary to say that as the Sacred Arch Masons had to erect their work within the temple, upon holy ground, they wore their hats, removed their shoes from off their feet; and as stated I. Kings vi. 7, were not allowed to use "any tool of iron" in the house.

Spon's "Dictionary of Engineering" describes an arch as "a form of structure in which the vertical forces, due to the weight of the material of which it is composed, are transmitted to the supports." However, many thousands of years ago the ancient Guild Masons employed three ways of constructing arches—(1) The ordinary method of "skew-backs," "voussoirs," and a "keystone." (2) The system in which each side of the arch is cut out of one piece of stone or marble, and keyed with a key stone, or three pieces in all. (3) The method of cutting out the whole arch complete so that it could be lifted up into position in one piece.

Arches are found in Babylon, Nineveh, also in Chinese bridges of great antiquity, and investigations prove that in one of the Egyptian pyramids, the "Hawara," there is an arched top to the sarcophagus chamber.

One of the oldest Arch Masons' Guilds in Egypt has in its possession inscriptions on tablets of stone which prove that the science of building stone arches came to them from Babylon.

One authority (Wilkinson) considered that the arched chambers of the Pyramids at Memphis carried the antiquity of the arch back to 2,600 B.C. The stone arch at Saqqara is of the period 600 B.C., and the stone arches of the tombs of Beni Hassan are coeval with Usertensen II. and the Viceroy Joseph.

"Bow" is the name of a very ancient instrument which consisted of a large arch of ninety degrees graduated. From an ancient building guild the writer finds that Bow Church, London, was built by arch stone masons, known as "Companions of the Arch Guild." It was designed by the Master of their Guild and was considered a masterpiece of arch-tect.

The "Treasury of Science" (Maunder) states that the Court of Arches is the Supreme Court belonging to the Archbishop of Canterbury, and that the name originated from the Court having been held in Bow Church, which was built on arches.

Haydn's "Dictionary of Dates," states:—"Arches, Court of, the most ancient consistory court; it derives its name from the Church of St. Mary-le-Bow, London, where it was formerly held, and whose top is raised on stone pillars and built archwise."

A "Bow Carpenter" or Centre Maker was a trade to itself, and the members belonged to the Bow Makers' Guild, but worked very closely with the Arch Masons, as their work was to construct the bow or centre of wood upon which the Arch Mason built his voussoirs, and finally, when he had completed the arch and put in the key stone, the "Bow Carpenter" removed the "centre." As previously mentioned the ancient Arch Masons measured their work by "circumference" "circular" or "round about" measure; for instance, we read I. Kings vii. 15, that at the time of Solomon's temple two pillars of brass were cast, "and a line of twelve cubits did compass either of them about." In the II. Chronicles iv. 2, we find that a molten sea was cast "and a line of thirty cubits did compass it round about."

The unit of the

ANCIENT HEBREW CIRCULAR MEASURE

was a circle having a circumference of one cubit.

As the royal cubit of Solomon was equal to our English 1.824 foot, it follows that a circle having a diameter of barely 7 inches will give the one circular cubit in circumference. Consequently if we examine a clock face having a diameter of 7 inches we have the Hebrew circular measure. Each minute of time, and each minute of distance, will then be one and the same in length, that is, very similar to our present three-eighths of an inch. Taking 12 o'clock as "0" we then find that 1 o'clock equals 30 degrees; 2, 60; 3, 90; 4, 120; 5, 150; 6, 180; 7, 210; 8, 240; 9, 270; 10, 300; 11, 330; 12, 360. It is a very interesting fact that this table of hours and angles has been discovered cut on stone both in Babylon and in Egypt, and it is preserved by the Arch Masons Guilds in England.

To illustrate the importance of the ancient

circular measure the writer by the courtesy of a member of a Masons' Company was able to give a table which related to the English foot. In practice there are many cases in which it is of value to be able to take the circumference and have the diameter worked out ready, in the same way that the Babylonians did thousands of years ago.

Before closing the details relating to the "Square" and the "Arch" Masons it should be added that two chairs about 250 years old are preserved at the Leicester Corporation Museum, the one has belonged to the Operative Square Guild, and the other to the Arch Guild—both of which guilds met at the White Lion Hotel, Leicester.

SETTING OUT THE CENTRE AND THE CORNERS.

A King or Ruler in ancient times having decided to construct a temple, public building, or pyramid, on a day arranged, attended in state at midday, and at the moment when the sun shone through an aperture fixed in the south, a proper signal was given that it was XII. o'clock noon.

Then with the usual ceremony of the period the "centre stone" was laid by the King, who also with a centre-punch made the centre mark upon the stone, at the same time remarking "There is the centre of the intended structure, work ye to it."

The ancient buildings were usually constructed of one of three forms—(1) Square. (2) Oblong—2 to 1. (3) Oblong 3 to 1.

SQUARE BUILDINGS.

If the building required was to be square, or to have a square-base, as in the case of a pyramid, the King decided upon the size and gave the distance measured from the centre A to each of the four corners F, G, H, I.

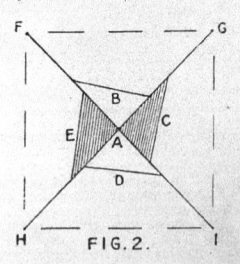

FIG. 2.

The length of the sides followed as a matter of course, but it was not considered in the laying out, which was simply based on the centre and four corner points.

Ancient tradition informs us that "6 times 60 equal to 360 Egyptian cubits was the length of the great pyramid from the centre to the corners, and modern experts estimate the length from the centre as 540 feet, which will give a diameter of 1,080 feet.

The ancient three Master Masons by means of their 3, 4, 5 rods, would then, from the centre struck by the King, form four right angled triangles and place the "pegs" to mark the position of the corners.

As the pegs at the corners would be probably moved or disturbed, the ancient Masons as long ago as the days of Babylon adopted

LANDMARKS.

They saw in those early days that if the pegs at the corners were moved the whole setting out of the work thus far would have to be repeated, therefore they adopted "land-lines" which extended to a considerable distance beyond the actual site of the structure. The land marks were pegs stuck into the ground at such a distance that they would not be disturbed, and it was the duty of every Guild Mason to take great care that these ancient land marks of the order were carefully preserved—in fact in the days of Solomon it was death to move a Free Mason's land mark or land line.

As mentioned previously, the ancients set out the ground plan of their square buildings by the distance from the centre to the four corners, and they proved the correctness of their work by the "land lines" and "land marks," also they measured the four angles at the centre, each of which of course must in the case of a square building be 90 degrees or the fourth part of a square.

OBLONG BUILDINGS, TWO TO ONE.

In the case of oblong structures built in the proportion of 40 by 20, or two to one, the ancient masons used the same "five point system," but the angle between the diagonal lines at the centre of a building having its length equal to twice its width, is 53.08 degrees as shown. The 53.08 degrees angle of the "3, 4, 5" square being used (A).

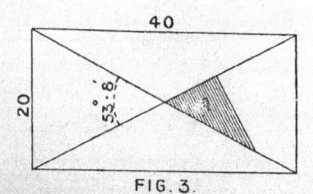

FIG. 3.

OBLONG BUILDINGS, THREE TO ONE.

All ancient temples in all parts of the world were constructed with the main hall or nave three times as long as the width or in the three to one proportion, and the height of the wall was "half the length."

King Solomon's temple was built exactly to this ancient mason's standard, for we read I. Kings vi. 2, "And the house which King Solomon built for the Lord, the length thereof was threescore cubits, the breadth thereof twenty cubits, and the height thereof thirty cubits." This proportion, cut upon stone tablets which have been discovered in Babylon and in Egypt, show that the ancients were fully aware that the angle at the centre formed by a three to one temple is equal to 36 degrees, 52 minutes.

The 36 degrees 52 minutes angle of the Master's square being employed as illustrated (B).

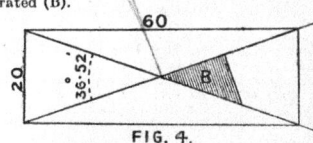

FIG. 4.

It is an interesting fact that many cathedrals and churches in England at the present day have been constructed on the three to one proportion used for temples in Babylon, India, Egypt, and Jerusalem.

The ancient Guild Masons in their records and "traditional history" explain that the reason why they had so much veneration for this proportion, is that the throne of their three Grand Masters had three seats, and rested upon a three to one basis.

From the above illustrations it will be seen that the three angles of the same "Master's square" were used for the laying out of the three forms of building, and it is easy therefore to understand the reason why the building trade secret of laying out on the centre was then preserved by the various "guilds" and "castes."

FOOTING STONES.

In order to give increased bearing surface upon the earth, every building and wall has "wide footings," that is the footing is made considerably wider than the wall or structure which has to rest upon it, and in all the ancient temples and important buildings "footing stones" were used for the foundations. These stones were of great size and weight being in cross section very similar to the letter L back to back.

"Footing stones" are well understood by all Installed Masters at the present day, as upon their aprons they have three cross sections of these ancient stones.

The four "corner footing stones" were of similar cross-section but formed the angle at each corner, and those used in the temple of King Solomon were of great size, as the dimensions work out as equal to a weight of no less than 45 tons each.

In the case of very large blocks of stone, such, for instance, as the corner footing stone of a temple, the ancients undermined the huge block of stone in the quarry, so that rollers could be placed under it. Therefore, when the stone was completely cut out it rested upon rollers, and did not have to be lifted. On arrival at the site of the building the stone was rolled on to a stage of timber constructed in the space for the foundation. The stone was then "eased up" sufficiently to enable the stage to be pulled away to the side, and the block was lowered into its position. So it will be seen that in the case of "footing stones" there was very little lifting necessary.

THE NORTH EAST CORNER.

It is a well known fact that at the present time, and also for thousands of years past, the first or foundation stone is always laid at the North East corner of the intended structure, and the question is frequently asked "Why do you begin at the N.E. any more than at any other corner?"

From the very earliest times, the answer to this question has been carefully preserved as one of the important Trade secrets of Guild Master Masons, but quite recently investigations at Babylon have led to the discovery of inscriptions which give the "reason" in full. As the information has already been made public in Egypt it is no longer a "Trade secret" and the Guilds and Companies of Masons have themselves communicated the following details.

To commence the actual building, the "land lines" must be tightly stretched between the respective "land marks," and at the points of intersection of the four outside "lines," the outside corners of the tops of the four great footing stones must be placed. To place these corners exactly correctly is of the very greatest importance as upon their correctness depends the whole work of erecting. Consequently the best possible light is required to see that the "footing stones" are placed "true to the land lines." The ancient Masons were quite well aware that the best possible light they could have upon the outside of their corner stones was "that great light of heaven," the sun, at the four periods of the day.

THE POSITION OF SOLOMON'S TEMPLE.

The door or "Enter-ance" to the Temple

of King Solomon, by which the ancients entered, was at the east end of the structure, and the north-east corner footing stone was laid near to the door on the left side of the building, as viewed by a person within the Temple.

THE THRONE IN THE WEST.

The most holy place, the inner courts, the King's throne, and the chancel were all at the west end of the building. The King, the High Priests, and others who were entitled to sit within the sacred chancel-arch, faced the east; but those who only had the right to sit in the nave or body of the Temple faced the west, and worshipped towards the most holy place.

The right or left hand side of the Temple always refers to the right or left of the King as he sat upon his throne in the west and faced the east, and this is made quite clear II. Chronicles iv, 10: "And he set the sea on the right side of the east end, over against the south."

In the same way we find that in all the ancient Building Guilds and Masons' Companies, in all parts of the world, the Three Masters are always placed in the west, so that they may see the rising sun in the east. An official is placed in the north to watch the sun at its meridian, and another officer sits in the east, so that he can watch the sun set in the west.

THE FOUNDATION OF THE TEMPLE.

From II. Chronicles iii., also from I. Kings vi., and from the Guild Masons' records, we find that Solomon began to build the temple on Mount Moriah, on the second day of the second month, Zif, which is equal to our month of May, at which time there would be ample sun-light.

At 6 o'clock in the morning Grand Master Mason Solomon began to lay the great North East corner footing stone, because at that time the sun-light was at the outside of the N.E. corner stone. That stone having been "well and truly laid to the land-lines," he proceeded at 10 o'clock to the South East corner and laid the S.E. corner stone as the sun at that time was shining at that corner. After refreshments, he proceeded to the South West corner and there laid the S.W. corner footing stone at 2 o'clock, by which time the sun was shining from the South West, and finally about 5 o'clock he proceeded to the North West corner and laid the N.W. corner stone. Thus it will be seen that the course of the sun was the reason why they commenced the temple at the N.E. corner and worked round to the North West. The four corners being thus "fixed" the work of laying all the intermediate "Footing stones" was carried out by Passed Masters or members of the sixth degree.

When the complete oblong foundation of footing stones was in position, the members of the Red Smiths' Guild arrived and placed "double taus of bronze" in the recesses which had been cut for them at the joints of the stones. Then the Plumb-smiths guild, "ran in the taus with melted lead." Thus the foundation was firmly held together, and all visitors to the East at the present day find at Babylon, in Egypt and in Rome the tau marks cut in the ancient stones, but unfortunately most of the bronze taus have been removed.

As soon as the row of footing stones was in position, the ancient Carpenters' Guild erected at the centre and at each corner, "stanchions of wood," and from each of these a plumb-line and plumb-bob was suspended respectively, exactly over the centre which the King had struck, and over the corners. From the centre plumb line the four corners were kept true until the work was completed. It was a well-known maxim that "if they kept true to the centre the corners could not err." It will, of course, be understood that the original centre stone remained in position, and a means was left to get to it in order to ascertain that the work was being carried out "dead upright," and on the "five point system."

Every day the "Super-Intendent" of Works tested the work from the centre, and at twelve o'clock at noon reported to the Grand Masters that "the work is true to the centre."

The ancient Guild Masons were wonderfully particular as to carrying out the work

COURSE BY COURSE.

That is they would not allow any stone of the second course to be laid until the whole of the footing stones were in position, nor might a third course be laid until the second course was completed.

At all the corners the ancients used "corner or angle stones" in the form of a letter L. These were of two sizes known as "long corner" and "short corner," the object being that when built up alternately, "they broke the joint," exactly in the same way that any bricklayer to-day avoids straight joints one over another.

The top row of stones in all ancient temples was formed of head, cope, or capestones, and they were usually twice the size of the ordinary stones.

The Guilds in Jerusalem and in Egypt have an ancient record that when the temple of Solomon was nearly completed and nothing remained but according to ancient custom for the King to lay the great North East "corner-head-stone" that by some error in the "marking" it was sent to the wrong stone-yard on the site of the building, and as it was not wanted there, it was "rejected."

After some delay, the rejected stone was found upon an Arch Guilds' rubbish-heap. The Square Guild Masons soon had it conveyed to its proper place, and thus "the stone which was rejected by the Arch

Masons was ultimately laid by Solomon and actually as a fact became the head-stone of the North East corner." The fixing of this head-stone, and also the fixing of the white marble key-stone within the temple, completed the structure ready for the dedication ceremony which is clearly described I. Kings viii.

LIFTING STONE.

Frequently we hear the question asked: How did the ancient stone-masons raise the enormous blocks of stone which they used in their temples and pyramids to the heights and positions in which they are now found?

frames C, and when 50 tons had been placed at the two ends, of course the stone was in perfect balance, and a few pounds placed on one side or the other would raise or lower the stone as the Master in charge might wish.

If stones of very great weight had to be raised, such for instance, as 1,000 tons, then the levers were made with their outer arms two, three, four, or five times longer than the inner ones. Thus the Ancients obtained enormous power, and with levers of three to one in favour of the power, it follows that 167 tons upon the two end scales at C would lift 1,000 tons in the centre, D.

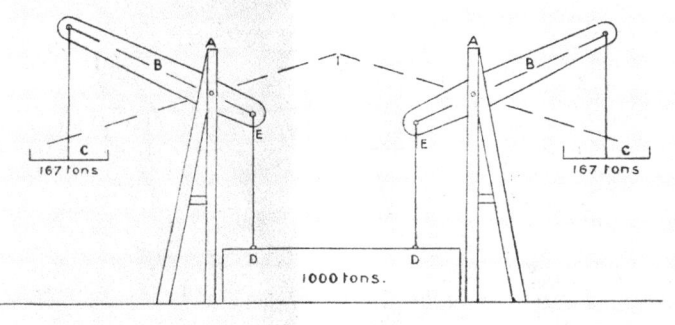

FIG. 1.

It is a very fortunate fact that the present Guild Masons have full details in China, India, and Egypt which clearly show how the work was carried out. The Carpenters' Guild constructed very strong uprights of timber A, and upon these they placed strong levers B, one end of the lever at E was attached to the stone at D, and the other end was attached to a frame-work upon which weights could be placed—C. To make the system clear we will take two pairs of ordinary scales, of the same size, and place them in a line, with say two feet between them. Place a board of say 2ft. 6in. in length so that the ends rest upon the two inner scales. If the board which represents the weight to be lifted weighs say 2lbs., it follows that if we place a one pound weight in the scale at each end, the "board" will be in perfect "balance." Then half an ounce weight added to or taken from the end scales will either raise or lower the board at our pleasure.

It is a most remarkable fact that this simple matter of "balancing" is fully explained and illustrated on tablets of burnt clay found in Babylon.

If it was necessary to lift a stone of, say, 100 tons, a gang of men was engaged to carry up weights and place them on the

The stone having been raised a few feet, blocks of wood were placed under it; the levers were returned to the former position, the chains shortened, and the process was repeated. Slowly, but surely, the ancient stonemasons lifted great weights to any height by this system. In those days there was unlimited labour and an ample number of men to carry up the necessary weights.

For light lifting they frequently employed the dead weight of men. Twenty men weigh one ton, and 100 men five tons, so if they sent up 100 men to the ends of the two levers it follows that they would raise ten tons without any trouble.

It is very fortunate that the Ancients cut on stone in Egypt, India, and the Holy Land the details of all their methods, so that we, thousands of years later, can clearly see how they carried out their work.

The above details show at a glance that the Ancient Free Masons had a perfect knowledge of levers and balance weights, and they had great knowledge of "wood craft," or they could never have designed the stanchions and balance beams capable of lifting 1,000 tons weight.

12 TECTONIC ART

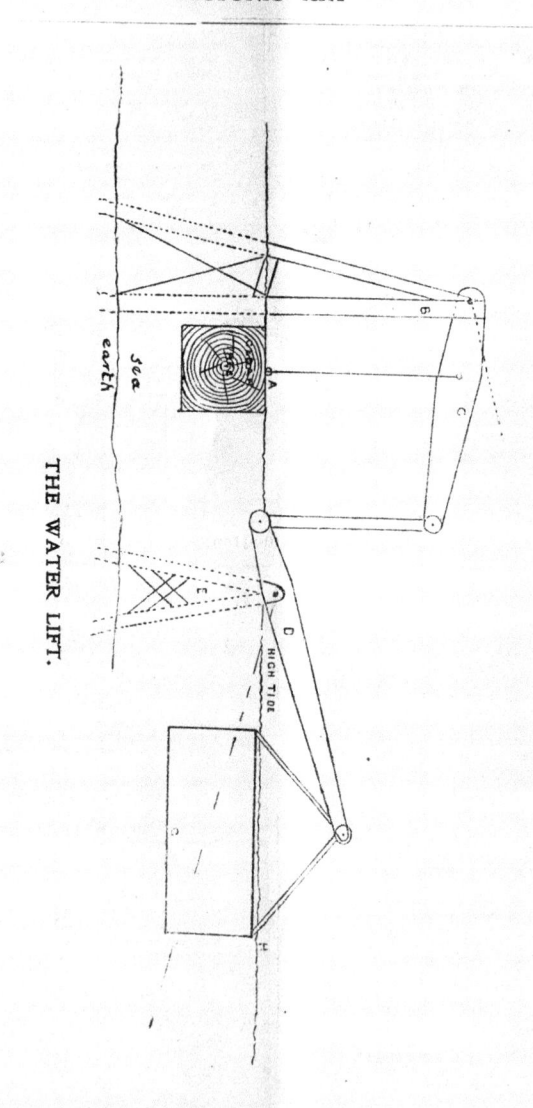

THE WATER LIFT.

If a river or a brook ran near, the Ancients made use of it, and let the water run into tanks, at the end of their levers, and at the sea side, and also in Egypt, they used the rise and fall of the tide. These were known as "the water lifts," and practically are the same as if we place the tray of a pair of scales under a tap of water, for as soon as the dead weight of the water at the one end, exceeded the weight of the load at the other the load must rise, no matter if the load be a pound, a ton, or a thousand tons.

THE WATER LIFT.

This form of "lift" was used on the River Nile, also in India, thousands of years ago; also at other sea coasts to raise timber, and was a very simple and mechanical appliance.

At the Egyptian Hall Exhibition of July, 1888, a model was shown of which the annexed diagram is a copy, and a similar model was at the Chicago Exhibition of 1893. A, is the tree to be lifted. B, the staunchion erected in the sea a short distance from the shore. C, a lever of the second order. E, Another staunchion, which carries D, a lever of the first order. F, a connecting-road between the two levers. G, a large tank capable of holding a vast weight of water, and open at the top.

All being ready, the tide rose to H, and the sea filled the tank G. When the tide went down, the tank of water went down, and the cedar tree was raised, and was then supported or "blocked up" until a further lift could be made.

At the conclusion of the first lift, a plug, or door, was opened in the tank, the water, was released, and the tank placed again in the position shown. The chain from C to A was shortened, and the process repeated.

If the tide did not rise sufficiently, or the timber was required to be raised quickly, the ancient "Intendent" in charge of the lifting called up a few hundred "carriers of water," and instructed them to carry up water and fill the tank.

In those days there was unlimited labour, and an ample number of men to carry up the necessary weights to the platforms, and when "water lifts" were worked by the rise and fall of the sea it sometimes happened that the work was required to be done quickly, the Task Master would then set a few hundred men to carry buckets of water to place in the tank and provide the lifting power.

As previously mentioned, the Guilds of Free Masons would not include or associate with quarrymen, they looked upon them as "some of those fourscore thousand hewers in the mountains." I. Kings v. 15. Free Masons were not allowed to touch a "rough-hewing tool" or 28lb. pointed or "scabbling" hammer. "Cowan" is the name of the man who "rough hewes," and who builds the stone walls between fields in North Wales, Derbyshire, etc., simply by "packing up"

rough broken stone. If a Free Mason is asked why he does not include the hewers in his Guild he will reply "My work is stone in courses, Cowan's work is stone out of course." To which the member of the "Hewers' Guild" will generally retort: "Where would you chaps be if we did not hew s.one for you."

THE ROUGH HEWERS.

The Hewers Guild in ancient times certainly did some wonderful work, for instance they quarried single blocks of stone which before being "dressed" weighed at least 1,100 tons. To get out such vast blocks they first undermined the stone from one end to the other and then placed rollers under it. Then at the back they cut out some hundreds or square holes, into each of which they dropped down a wedge of wood with the wide end downwards, then they put in a second wedge with the thin end downwards, this system being known as

HEWERS' DOUBLE WEDGING

and was of course one of their trade secrets. Then three powerful men with heavy setting mauls commenced to drive down every one of the uppermost wedges as far as they could, and it was quite usual for 500 or 800 of the strikers to be employed on this work at one time. Then the "carriers of water" were sent for, and they filled all the holes with water. In time the expansion of the wedges caused the 1,100 ton stone to burst out, and it then rested on the rollers ready for the "haulers" and some of those "three score and ten thousand that bare burdens" (I. Kings v. 15) to come and haul it out of the quarry, and take it to the No. 1 Square Mason's stoneyard for the apprentices to begin upon.

In various parts of the world there are most wonderful examples of

PREHISTORIC GUILD WORK.

One of the most wonderful places is the Indian Madura Temple. There is a door like a tunnel that pierces through a huge pyramid of gods that towers into the sky. Then is reached the temple itself, a silent and echoing city, whose vaulted streets cross one another in all directions, and whose countless people are the stone images graven here. Each column and each monstrous pillar is made of a single block, placed upright by means of the "lifts" previously described, and afterwards deeply sculptured and carved into images of all sorts of gods and monsters. Again, in the grottos of Siva, the god of death, near Go.conda, are courts hewn out of the solid granite, and of troops of carved elephants which form the supports of a triple sequence of monolithic temples. Truly a wondrous land, bespeaking a barbaric civilization and splendour at a period when England had hardly come into being. Another perfect piece of prehistoric architecture is the wonderful "mosaic chamber," situated among the famous ruins of the ancient city of Mitla, thirty miles south of the city of Mexico. Although months have been spent by prominent travellers, writers and archæologists in the attempt to read the history of this old city from the hieroglyphics yet visible on its walls, the only thing known to-day of Mitla or its buildings, of architecture, of temples and palaces, is grouped on a slight elevation besides a narrow stream. Even the name of Mitla is of unknown origin. But while every structure of which this group is composed is covered within and without with mosaics, it remains for the great Hall known as the "mosaic chamber" to reveal the work at its best. The marvellous part is that there is not a single piece of tile missing from the entire room. These mosaics were put together without the aid of cement or mortar.

Some portion of the ruins of Mitla had been covered with sand for unknown centuries when the Mexican government began excavating, but the larger portion of the buildings were above the ground, exposed to the elements. About two hundred and seventy-five years ago one of the Mitla temples was pulled down, and a church built with the stone. This the natives call the "new church," although it is nearly three hundred years old.

Beneath one of the temples of Mitla an underground chamber has been found, and under this is believed to be another subterranean room, which the Mexican government is now taking steps to investigate. It is fully expected that the old Guild method of building from a "centre plumb line" will be found in this lower room, and great interest is being taken in the matter.

One of the most sacred shrines of India, which had been for centuries the goal of pilgrimages from all parts of India, was the great temple of Ramesvara, sacred to Rama, situated on an island close to the mainland, in the channel between South India and Ceylon. It had a magnificent Gopuram. Its most striking feature, however, was the wonderful corridors which adorned it. The south corridor was 700ft. in length, that is to say, it was the longest in the world except that in the Vatican. The most attractive of all the Chalukyan shrines was the great temple of Siva at Halebid, about twenty miles from Belun, built on a terrace slanting down to the lake.

In the year 1270 A.D. it was left unfinished, and the towers have never been completed. It was one of the most remarkable monuments in India. One of the pavilions in front contained a huge image of the Bull of Siva. In the interior were some remarkable black stone pillars, which looked as if they had been turned in a lathe. This temple was unmatched in the variety of its details and the exuberance of fancy shown in its ornamentation. There is, perhaps, no other temple in the world on the outside carving of which such a marvellous amount of graving has been performed. It will give some idea of the enormous amount of sculpture with which this temple was covered when it is mentioned that the lowest band of the frieze alone contained a procession of about 2,000 elephants, no two of which are exactly alike.

Now turning to the wonders of Egypt, in one of the caverns at Memphis there are numerous sarcophagi in granite blocks, weighing from 60 to 80 thousand kilos—says a French writer. Mariette Bey endeavoured to get one of the smallest of them removed. But all his efforts only enabled him to draw the monolith a little further towards the passage.

Over the top of the door of Solomon's temple there was placed a very long and large "head-stone" or lintel. It contained no less than 60 cube cubits of stone, and was regarded as the height of Square Mason's tectonic Art. This stone, which was placed in position by the King, had "graved" upon it, in Hebrew characters, the first words of that Holy Book:

"IN THE BEGINNING GOD CREATED

THE HEAVEN AND THE EARTH."

The letters themselves were of solid gold, and let into the graved part of the stone. It was, therefore, indeed, a work of art worthy of the King, the nation, the masons, and the goldsmiths' guild.

After investigations one can only come to the conclusion that years ago in the Guild days there were some wonderfully clever men engaged in the ancient system.

In England, St. Paul's Cathedral was commenced in the year 1675, by the St. Paul's Guild of Free Masons, the stone being made ready at Portland and sent to London by water.

THE GUILDS IN ENGLAND DECLINE.

In 1710 the Rev. James Anderson was the Chaplain of the St. Paul's Guild Masons, who, at that time, had their head quarters at the Goose and Gridiron Ale-house in St. Paul's churchyard, London, and in September, 1714, the books of the Guild shew that Anderson had made a very remarkable "innovation" in the rules, which was, to admit persons as members of the Masons' Guild without their serving the seven years' apprenticeship. This caused a split in the ranks. Many of the Masters and Passed Masters of the Guilds in various parts of the country joined the new system of Dr. Anderson.

At the White Lion Hotel, Leicester, for instance, a Guild had existed for a very long period, but in 1790 the chief members became members of the system of Anderson, termed by the Guilds "Andersonry." At a later date the workmen of the lower grades all decided that they would not continue to work under the Guild system, and no boys would serve the seven years' apprenticeship.

Soon after the Trade Union Act of 1871 was passed, the new "Stonemasons' Trade Union," took over as members a large majority of the Guild members, and at the present time although Masons' Companies and Guilds exist in England the writer is not aware that any stone-yard since 1883 has been managed and controlled upon the ancient Guild system of the Free Masons.

In conclusion the writer may say that for thousands of years guilds have carried out the most strict letter of the law not to allow outsiders to obtain the very "least trace" of the ancient systems; but now several of them have decided that it is perfectly lawful to have the "bare facts" of their history written by their own respective officials. It must therefore be understood that the recent articles in the *Melton Times* are not by any means the complete history, but only so much as the writer has received authority to make known to the readers.

BV - #0054 - 030823 - C0 - 210/148/3 - PB - 9780853186441 - Matt Lamination